# THE CHICANO MOVEMENT

# THE CHICANO MOVEMENT

## *A Historical Exploration of Literature*

**Sara E. Martínez**

HISTORICAL EXPLORATIONS OF LITERATURE

 GREENWOOD™

An Imprint of ABC-CLIO, LLC
Santa Barbara, California • Denver, Colorado

**Library of Congress Cataloging-in-Publication Data**

Names: Martínez, Sara E.
Title: The Chicano movement : a historical exploration of literature / Sara E. Martínez [author]
Description: Santa Barbara, California : Greenwood, an imprint of ABC-CLIO, LLC [2017] | Series: Historical explorations of literature | Includes bibliographical references and index.
Identifiers: LCCN 2016041924 (print) | LCCN 2016054995 (ebook) | ISBN 9781610697071 (acid-free paper) | ISBN 9781610697088 (e-book)
Subjects: LCSH: American literature—Mexican American authors—History and criticism. | Chicano movement. | Mexican Americans—Social conditions.
Classification: LCC PS153.M4 C475 2017 (print) | LCC PS153.M4 (ebook) | DDC 810.9/86872—dc23
LC record available at https://lccn.loc.gov/2016041924

ISBN: 978-1-61069-707-1
EISBN: 978-1-61069-708-8

21  20  19  18  17    1  2  3  4  5

This book is also available as an eBook.

Greenwood
An Imprint of ABC-CLIO, LLC

ABC-CLIO, LLC
130 Cremona Drive, P.O. Box 1911
Santa Barbara, California 93116-1911
www.abc-clio.com

This book is printed on acid-free paper ∞
Manufactured in the United States of America

Para Alma, José Emiliano, y la próxima generación—a Liliana, Victoria y Sylvia

# Contents

# Series Foreword

The Historical Explorations of Literature series is designed to help students understand key works of American literature by putting them in the context of history, society, and culture through historical context essays, literary analyses, chronologies, primary source documents, and suggestions for further research. Each volume in the series covers four or five canonical works related to a particular area of American literature—significant literary productions of the Jazz Age or the Harlem Renaissance, for example. For each title covered, students will find a brief synopsis of the work; separate essays on the work's historical background and the author's biographical background; an essay on "Why We Read This Work," summarizing the work's enduring value and significance; and a series of thematic "Historical Explorations" that include a selection of related primary documents.

# Preface

The Chicano movement took place during the turbulent 1960s, a time when oppressed people in the United States and around the world found and exercised their power. In the United States, African Americans led the way, soon to be followed by Chicanos, American Indians, women, and others. They tested their strength by following the nonviolent strategies of Gandhi and Martin Luther King, Jr.; they found strength in solidarity, working together across racial and class lines. It was a heady time as their power brought real change to their communities and a hope that they could aspire to a dignified standard of living.

The Chicano movement was born in the frustration and humiliation of veterans who had served their country only to be barred from businesses who would not serve Mexicans or dogs; it was born from the sweat, toil, blood, and tears of farmworkers who had been exploited and abused for too long; it was born in the thirst for justice of a people who had lost their land and been shunted off to the *barrios*; it was born of women finding themselves the victims of forced sterilization; it was born in the rage of high school students fed up with crumbling schools and teachers who denigrated their culture. It was nurtured by solidarity; by the courage to face beatings, imprisonment, and repression together; by wild creativity in music and literature; and by incremental successes and great challenges—marches, eloquent speeches, moratoriums, and *solidaridad*.

This book aims to present a holistic picture of the Chicano movement from the perspective of Chicano literature. The novels selected were written by authors from different regions of Aztlán, with different life experiences and world views although, of course as Chicanos, these life experiences and cultural values overlap.

The *abuelito* of Chicano letters, Rudolfo Anaya of New Mexico, embodies the Southwestern perspective of the Chicano who has inhabited that part of the country since before the Pilgrims landed on Plymouth Rock. His novel *Bless Me, Ultima* speaks to the Chicanos' deep spiritual roots and historical claims on this land. Born in Texas, author Tomás Rivera lived the life of a migrant farmworker up until he entered junior college. His novel *This Migrant Earth* portrays that itinerant, insecure, hardworking way of life of families from Texas throughout the Midwest and California. The iconic Oscar Z. Acosta was born in California and also worked in the fields as a child. His novel *The Revolt of the Cockroach People* depicts the frenetic and exhilarating beginnings of the Chicano movement in Los Angeles. From the Midwest, Sandra Cisneros set her transcendent novel *The House on Mango Street* in a barrio of Chicago. With a young girl's voice, the book powerfully narrates the Chicana experience.

The Chicano movement positively changed the status quo for many, and political representation has improved at every level from Congress to the Cabinet and even a Latina on the Supreme Court. The struggle continues into the 21st century as we battle many of the same issues that roused Aztlán over 50 years ago including voting rights, crumbling schools, abuse by law enforcement, negative stereotypes, and exploitation of undocumented workers.

I have been told that no one calls themselves "Chicano" anymore and queried The Mexican about this in his syndicated advice column. He assures me that:

> the fact is that "Chicano" as an identity was endangered by the 1980s, under assault from the Right by *vendidos* who preferred "Hispanic" and by Mexican immigrants who taught their children they were *mexicanos*, not *pocho*-ass Chicanos. [. . .] The super-mega-anti-immigrant rhetoric . . . is so nasty that an even newer identity is emerging: Xicanx. (Arellano, 2016)

For the purposes of this book, I have used Chicano, Mexican, and Mexican American almost interchangeably, generally noting any exceptions. In any case, *si son peras o manzanas, todos somos hermanas/os/x. . .*
### *¡Viva la raza!*

## Reference

Arellano, Gustavo. (2016, March 24). "Is the Term 'Chicano' Endangered?" *OC Weekly*. http://www.ocweekly.com/news/is-the-term-chicano-endangered -7061743.

# Acknowledgments

Many thanks/*muchísimas gracias y cariño* to my dad Joe Martínez for his patience and *apoyo*; to my *carnala* Mary Martínez and *buen amiga*, Marianne Stambaugh for their meticulous and thoughtful feedback. I am grateful to my librarian colleagues: Jessica Reed in Tulsa provided invaluable research support and Daniel Hernández at the Chicano Resource Center of the East Los Angeles Library helped with access to early Teatro Campesino texts (gracias to *amigo y camarada* Jaime García Villalobos for that contact). I owe an enormous *deuda* to the Chicano Studies scholars and am grateful to Arturo Rosales for his handy compilation of documents from Chicano history—*Testimonio*. Thank heavens for the Interlibrary Loan Department at Tulsa City-County Library. Any errors are my own.

# Chronology

<table>
<tr><td>1492</td><td>Columbus lands in Cuba.</td></tr>
<tr><td>1510</td><td>Cortez lands in Vera Cruz; recruits Malinalli later known as La Malinche to be his interpreter.</td></tr>
<tr><td>1610</td><td>La Villa Real de la Santa Fe de San Francisco de Asís is designated the capital of the province of Nuevo México, making it the oldest state capital in the United States.</td></tr>
<tr><td>1651</td><td>Juana Inés de Asbaje y Ramírez de Santillana is born in San Miguel Nepantla, New Spain. She takes the name Sor Juan Inés de la Cruz on becoming a nun.</td></tr>
<tr><td>1810</td><td>La Corregidora Josefa Domínguez de Ortiz conspires with insurgents against Spanish rule.<br><br>Mexico wins independence from Spain.</td></tr>
<tr><td>1835</td><td>Father Antonio José Martínez publishes El Crepúsculo in New Mexico, the first Spanish language newspaper in the United States.</td></tr>
<tr><td>1848</td><td>U.S.–Mexico War ends and the California gold rush begins.</td></tr>
</table>

1910    Mexican revolution takes place.

1912    New Mexico and Arizona are ratified as states #47 and 48.

1913    Francisca Flores is born in San Diego.

1928    *Las aventuras de Don Chipote o Cuando los pericos mamen* is published in Los Angeles.

1929    The League of United Latin American Citizens is founded in Texas.

1934    Tomás Rivera is born in Crystal City, Texas.

1937    Rudolfo Anaya is born in Abiquiu, New Mexico.

1938    Emma Tenayuca organizes Pecan-Shellers in San Antonio.

1942    The U.S. and Mexican governments implement the *Bracero* program.

1943    The Zoot Suit riots take place in Los Angeles.

1946    *Mendez v. Westminster School District* trial makes segregation of Mexican children unconstitutional in California.

1948    The American G.I. Forum is established in Corpus Christi, Texas.

1952    The Salt of the Earth strike wins wage and other concessions from mine operators in Silver City, New Mexico.

1954    Operation Wetback is implemented.

        *Hernandez v. Texas* extends constitutional protection to Mexicans as a class.

        Sandra Cisneros is born in Chicago, Illinois.

1955    *Romance of a Little Village Girl* is published.

        *Barrio Boy* is published.

1957    Los Angeles begins removing Mexican American homeowners from Chavez Ravine, later to become Dodger Stadium.

1959    *Pocho* is published.

        Mexican American Political Association is founded to elect Mexican American candidates to public office.

1960    *Harvest of Shame* is aired on CBS after Thanksgiving.

1962    Cesar Chavez leaves the Community Service Organization (CSO) to form the National Farm Workers Association (NFWA).

1963    Mexican Americans win control of Crystal City, Texas, at the ballot box on the La Raza Unida Party ticket.

1964    *Bracero* program is suspended.

Agricultural Workers Organizing Committee (AWOC) strike against grape growers over wages.

1966    AWOC unites with the NFWA to form the United Farm Workers of America.

The UFW marches from Delano to Sacramento.

Young Citizens for Community Action (YCCA) is established in Los Angeles.

Corky Gonzales founds Crusade for Justice in Denver, Colorado.

United Farm Workers Union calls for a national boycott of grapes.

1967    *I Am Joaquin* is published.

Frito Lay launches Frito Bandido ad campaign.

Young Mexican American activists from Chicago, Colorado, New Mexico, Texas, and California meet with Tijerina in Albuquerque and plans for a National Youth Conference and a National party are born.

1968    Los Angeles Police Department officer Fernando Sumaya infiltrates the Brown Berets as agent provocateur.

The National Mexican American Anti-Defamation League is launched.

YCCA becomes the Brown Berets.

East Los Angeles School Blow Outs take place.

Cesar Chavez uses a hunger strike to emphasize nonviolence as UFW's preferred tactic.

1969    National Chicano Liberation Youth Conference takes place in Denver, Colorado.

Christmas Eve St. Basil Cathedral demonstration takes place.

Catolicos por La Raza is founded in Los Angeles.

Fires set at Biltmore Hotel in Los Angeles during Governor Reagan's speech; Biltmore 6 are indicted.

Former UCLA student body president Rosalío Muñoz, Sal Baldenegro of the University of Arizona, and Ernesto Vigil of the Crusade for Justice in Denver refuse induction and burn their draft cards.

1970    La Raza Unida Party is established.

UFW signs contract with grape growers.

Second Chicano Youth Conference takes place in Denver.

Informant and agent provocateur for the ATF Frank Martinez becomes chair of the Chicano Moratorium Committee.

Ruben Salazar is killed at the Chicano Moratorium, Laguna Park, Los Angeles.

Oscar Z. Acosta runs for sheriff of Los Angeles County on the La Raza Unida Party ticket.

1971    Frito Bandido ad campaign is canceled due to pressure from Chicano activist groups.

*. . . y no se lo trago la tierra* wins the first Quinto Sol prize.

Chicano Liberation Front bombings take place in Los Angeles.

Tijerina is released from prison.

Biltmore 6 are found not guilty.

National Chicana Conference is held in Houston.

1972    *Bless Me Ultima* wins Quinto Sol prize.

1973    *Revolt of the Cockroach People* is published.

1978    Chicanas in Los Angeles sue the USC/Los Angeles County Medical Center over coerced sterilization practices.

1979    Arte Público Press is founded by Dr. Nicolás Kanellos.

1981    *This Bridge Called My Back* is published.

1984    *The House on Mango Street* is published.

1999    Sandra Cisneros receives a MacArthur "genius grant" fellowship.

# 1

# *Bless Me, Ultima*
# **(1972)**

*New Mexico, with some 60,000 inhabitants, had a much larger population than many western territories that Congress admitted to statehood during the nineteenth century. Members of Congress were reluctant to admit a territory with a majority of Mexicans. In return, many Mexican villagers and Pueblo Indians resented the North American conquest and resultant encroachment on their land. Armed rebellion was common, with active resistance to the North American military occupation. In fact, the history of New Mexico explodes the myth that New Mexicans willingly became incorporated into the North American Union.*

—Rodolfo Acuña, *Freedom in a Cage: The Colonization of New Mexico* in *Occupied America*, 77

*The abiding character of New Mexico as a Catholic, hispanophone land delayed statehood. Congress turned down fifteen applications before the status was finally confirmed in 1912. (. . .) The decisive reasons for New Mexico's long exclusion, however, are clear: xenophobia verging on racism and a narrow-minded understanding of what it means to belong to the United States. (. . .) New Mexico became a state when the balance between Anglos and others tipped. Now the trends that prevailed since the United States seized the region have gone into reverse. Nearly half the people of the state are native speakers of Spanish. . . The state song is bilingual. The numbers of people of indigenous descent have recovered spectacularly.*

—Felipe Fernández-Armesto, *Our America*, 196–197

# SYNOPSIS

Written and published in the late 1960s/early 1970s, Rudolfo Anaya's classic novel *Bless Me, Ultima* is set in post—World War II northern New Mexico in a little pueblo called Las Pasturas. The novel is told in the voice of seven-year-old Antonio Marez: Antonio is the youngest son who lives with his mother, father, and two older sisters. When the book opens, his brothers have not yet returned from fighting in the war, and Antonio's parents have decided to take in the healing woman, Ultima, in her time of need. Although many in the pueblo fear her as a *bruja*/witch, the Marez family reveres her as a respected elder, someone to whom they owe a debt of gratitude as she is the midwife who delivered Antonio.

Antonio's family has lived in the region for generations from the time of the original Spanish land grants. They are devout Catholics and Antonio's mother hopes that he will grow up to be a priest. That pressure makes Antonio feel a responsibility toward others and also brings him to question and doubt his faith. His mother is a Luna ("moon" in English), who comes from a farming family and is tied to the land, while his father is a Marez ("seas" in English), a *vaquero* who yearns for change and the open range, hoping that, upon returning from World War II, his veteran sons will accompany him on a new adventure in California.

Antonio becomes Ultima's helper and accompanies her as she collects the roots and herbs needed for traditional remedies. She teaches him her craft, that of a *curandera*/healer, as well as mystical, magical, and spiritual lessons. She helps him work through the fear that comes from witnessing terrifying events, through his troubling dreams and his doubts about the nature of God.

The last year of Antonio's childhood recounted in *Bless Me, Ultima* is marked by four violent deaths. Lupito's is the first. Lupito has killed the sheriff while out of his mind from "shell-shock," reliving his time at the front fighting Japanese soldiers. Antonio's father is part of the group that chases Lupito, intending only to detain him but instead Lupito is shot and killed. Antonio had sneaked away to follow his father and watches the sequence of events from nearby, afraid that his father is one of those who fired on Lupito. Antonio is terrified but as he lies sobbing, he hears and is comforted by the sound of Ultima's familiar white owl.

Antonio attends church and school with a rough group of boys—Horse, Bones, Ernie, Able, Lloyd, Florence, and the Kid. They are all older than Antonio and like to swear and fight. Throughout this singular year, Antonio enters grade school and learns English, has a role in the Christmas play, prepares for first Communion and sees his brothers return home to Las Pasturas. They are not interested in their father's schemes and instead take on jobs and scandalous lovers. Antonio is confused by their behavior and searches for answers from religion, from the Virgin Mary, and later, from a golden carp.

Antonio learns of the divine golden carp from his friends Cico and Samuel. They tell him an origin story of primitive gods from the time when the earth was young. The golden carp manifests an ancient spirituality, ties to earthly wisdom, and elemental fears that speak powerfully to Antonio. He suffers intense crises of consciousness over his reverence for the golden carp and for Ultima's teachings that seem to exist in opposition to his parents' Catholic faith.

When his uncle Lucas is taken deathly ill after an encounter with a trio of unsavory witches at their black mass, Antonio's grandfather sends for Ultima. The evil sisters are Don Tenorio's daughters and they have put Lucas under a curse that is killing him. Ultima agrees to help, taking only Antonio with her. She confronts Tenorio and is able to save Lucas through her own magic, and the witches lose their power and ultimately perish, making Tenorio a mortal enemy of Ultima. Tenorio's first attempt on Ultima's life is unsuccessful; he whips up a drunken mob to accuse her of *brujería*/witchcraft but she survives, defended by the men in Antonio's family. (Antonio later finds evidence that she was able to pass their "witch" test by distracting them with her owl.)

Narciso is the next person Antonio watches die. He is the town drunk who hears Tenorio threaten to go to the Marez house to take revenge on Ultima. Antonio is walking home from school late (after rehearsal for the Christmas play) during a snow storm when he sees Narciso and Tenorio fighting. When Tenorio leaves, threatening to go after Antonio's family, Antonio follows Narciso. Narciso tries to roust Antonio's brother Andrew out of the whorehouse. It is a cold evening and Andrew's lover convinces him that Narciso is crazy and to stay out of the cold and close the door. Narciso proceeds to take it upon himself to warn the Marez family about Tenorio's evil intentions. On the way, he again encounters Tenorio who shoots him for his trouble; Tenorio also tries to shoot Antonio but misses and runs away. Antonio comforts Narciso as he is dying and Narciso prevails upon Antonio to hear his confession. When Antonio makes it home through the storm, disappointed in his brother, he succumbs to a fever and is cared for and protected by Ultima.

Florence's is the third death. Florence's hard life has extinguished his belief in God; he refuses to go to catechism and be confirmed as a Catholic. Antonio is troubled because he understands Florence's doubts since Antonio himself is drawn by the mystical, primal appeal of the golden carp and plans to bring Florence to see it and be initiated in its glory. Florence is bullied by the other kids who try to prevail on Antonio as the future priest to assign him a penance—to be beaten or killed for his nonbelief and heresy. Antonio refuses, "absolves" Florence, and is beaten in his place. Florence goes swimming later that day, dives into the deep, dangerous water, and drowns when he is caught on a piece of wire, never to know the golden carp. (Anaya had a similar experience during his 16th summer when he broke his neck in a diving accident.)

The final death that brings an end to Antonio's childhood is, of course, Ultima's. An outraged, drunken Tenorio finally carries out his threat, and while aiming at Antonio, shoots the white owl instead, which effectively kills Ultima. When he again has Antonio in his sights, Tenorio is shot by Antonio's uncle Pedro. Antonio buries the owl under the forked juniper tree in the moonlight, which he feels to be Ultima's true burial place, not the pine coffin in the cemetery. She blesses Antonio with her final words: "I bless you in the name of all that is good and strong and beautiful, Antonio. Always have the strength to live. Love life, and if despair enters your heart look for me in the evenings when the wind is gentle and the owls sing in the hills. I shall be with you" (276).

## HISTORICAL BACKGROUND: *BLESS ME, ULTIMA* AND THE NASCENT CHICANO CONSCIOUSNESS

Ultima's blessing uplifted a community in flux. Like the young Antonio, Chicanos were suffering the growing pains of a nascent consciousness. The generation that grew to maturity during the turbulent times of the 1960s questioned and challenged everything it had taken for granted while seeking to understand the trajectory of its history and roots. The budding Chicano movement took pride in the dual nature of Chicanos' origin—*ni de aquí ni de allá*/not from here nor from there; both Indian and European, both Mexican and American. Exploring that duality, Rudolfo Anaya encapsulates in *Bless Me, Ultima* the deep roots of the Chicano people in the Southwest while bringing to the fore the losses suffered during their long trajectory of struggle for survival. Anaya set *Bless Me, Ultima* in Las Pasturas, located in northern New Mexico. This region is a kind of ground zero for the original clash that gave birth to the Mexican American people, the Chicanos. Charles C. Mann in his book *1493* calls the transculturation process initiated by Columbus's arrival in Hispaniola the "Columbian Exchange." For Chicanos, the process began when the Spanish conquistadors landed in Veracruz on the Gulf of Mexico and continued as they searched for gold and glory throughout the continent. Juan de Oñate was the first conquistador to explore and initiate the exchange of what is now New Mexico.

*New* Mexico is actually old—old land, old culture. Its capital, Santa Fe, is the oldest capital city in the United States, having been founded in 1610 by the Spanish Crown some six years before the English established Jamestown as the capital of their American colonies. Jamestown is now mostly a tourist attraction while Santa Fe continues functioning as the seat of government in New Mexico. Studying New Mexican history (and that of the entire Southwestern United States) requires turning the generally held view (from the U.S. perspective) on its head, to contemplate Manifest Destiny from the receiving end. Manifest Destiny, that relentless march of Anglo "civilization" attempted to ride roughshod over centuries-old cultures. These established cultures were borne of the Columbian Exchange that had taken place between Spanish conquistadors and the native people whose descendants are the Chicanos living in the southwestern region of what is now the United States. In New Mexico, the conquerors' archaic Spanish is still spoken in some remote pueblos and people in Ácoma pueblo still commemorate the cruelty of Juan de Oñate who determined to subjugate the pueblo for daring to revolt against Spanish rule: he ordered that one hand be cut off every male between the ages of 12 and 25 and that the left foot be cut off every male 25 years old or older. Sixty young girls were sent to convents in Mexico City, never to return to Ácoma. The rest of the females were parceled out as servants to the colonists (Stavans, 77).

The Spanish conquest began in earnest in 1510 when Hernando Cortés burned his ships and began his march toward Tenochtitlan/Mexico City to conquer this "New World" for the Spanish Crown. He soon found he would have to vanquish the Aztecs who along with Texcoco and Tlacopan formed the Triple Alliance that ruled central Mexico. Their city of

Tenochtitlan was bigger and richer than any city in Spain (Mann, 282). The Aztecs themselves had come to Tenochtitlan from far away, from a mystical place in the hazy north called Aztlán according to their origin story. They arrived as starving outcasts, reduced to inhabiting that swampy place in central Mexico. From there, they built a vast and sophisticated empire and Tenochtitlan, a city on the lake—an engineering feat that rivaled Venice.

In the 1960s, the Chicanos claimed Aztlán, inspired by the Aztec origin story that mirrored their own. Chicanos were regarded as Mexican outcasts and looked down upon from all sides—from their country of origin and from their adopted country. From this lowly place, they resolved that great things would come as they channeled the Aztec spirit of strength, endurance, and ingenuity. Chicanos also shared with the Aztecs a history of invasion and abuse: as the Aztecs were robbed of their land, culture, and dominion by the Spanish, so the Chicanos were robbed of their land, culture, and dominion by the Anglo. Aztlán is the Chicano nation/*patria,* and although it has no physical or geographical boundaries, its spiritual center is in the Southwestern United States and its *compatriotas* are joined by solidarity, history, and cultural kinship.

Fast forward a few hundred years from the conquest and by the middle of the 19th century, Mexico had gained its independence at a high cost and continued to be subject to government by strongmen, generals, and dictators while struggling to implement a viable federalist system similar to the U.S. model. Meanwhile, northern Mexico/Southwestern United States had been sparsely populated. The communities in the wild, northern extremes of the Spanish Empire had been awarded large land grants or charters by the colonial bureaucracy and later by the Mexican government as an enticement to settle regions considered dangerous because of the hostility of native people[1] and the unforgiving desert environment. These were huge expanses of land that functioned like the *ejido* system in central Mexico: the land was owned communally, and the work as well as the fruits of their labor was shared by the community.

Anglo Americans intent on venturing across the continent to seek their fortune first came up against Mexicans and the Mexican government in Texas. The experience was qualitatively different than their usual strategy of pushing the native nations, tribes, and people out of their way. Although Mexico was struggling, it was a large country with an army that had defeated the Spanish and counted on international allies. Stephen F. Austin began the process by entering into a pact whereby Mexico agreed to let 400 Catholic families settle in *Tejas*. "This contract became a wedge that allowed thousands of other Anglos to flock into the region" (Rosales, 1). Once the Anglos had critical mass, they took their grievances (nonconformity with the Mexican Roman-style legal system, inaccessibility of federal government and services, lack of protection from marauding Comanche, etc.) to justify their demand for independence from Mexico. Mexico refused to acknowledge the independence of Texas and suspected the United States of instigating the move. These suspicions were confirmed when the United States annexed Texas in 1845. The United States then offered Mexico $25 million to buy the rest of the land north of the Rio Grande for Manifest Destiny purposes. When Mexico refused to even receive the negotiators, President James Polk ordered General Zachary Taylor to blockade the Rio Grande River. Mexico retaliated, resulting in U.S. casualties, and Polk got a declaration of war from Congress.

After Mexico lost its war with the United States in 1848, the two countries signed the Treaty of Guadalupe Hidalgo, which spelled out what was to become of the territories and the people living there who had previously been Mexican citizens, not including Texas. The treaty ceded more than half of Mexico's territory to the United States, encompassing New Mexico, Arizona, Nevada, California, Texas, parts of Utah, Colorado, and the Oklahoma panhandle. The United States paid Mexico only $15 million for more territory than it had tried to buy previously. Mexico made an effort to protect its erstwhile citizens with the concessions outlined in Article IX under threat of total annihilation of Mexico by the Polk administration. Dirty tricks accompanied the treaty negotiations and signing, a harbinger for later nonimplementation and lack of respect for the treaty. Mexican Americans lost over 20 million acres between the end of the war in 1848 and 1880.

This plunder was accomplished by the concentration of power in the hands of men appointed by Washington whose allegiance was to the new arrivals. These men monopolized the territorial legislature and controlled all levels of law enforcement as well as the banks. The land grabbers could set their sights on a piece of land and fence their claim. The railroads and the national park system took over grand swaths of land that were then closed off for grazing. The erstwhile Mexicans had little recourse; if they didn't pay the exorbitant taxes required to support the railroads, for example, their property was forfeited.

The Mexicans tried a variety of strategies to fight back. Some united to form mutual aid groups like the Knights of Labor. Some tried fighting in the courts although even if they won in court, the verdict was disregarded and the abuse continued. Some tried getting like-minded representatives elected to the legislature, which only ended in hopeless frustration. Others resorted to direct action under the cover of night. Such were *Las gorras blancas* established in 1887 by Juan José Herrera. *Las gorras blancas* would mount up in their long black slickers with pistols at the ready and their identity protected by white masks. They would spend the night cutting the fences that presented hated obstacles to grazing. They would attack the railroads and property of those they saw as enemies of the people. Their campaign stopped the land grabbing for only a couple of years before infiltrators and political infighting weakened the group.

Reies Lopez Tijerina resurrected the spirit of *Las gorras blancas* when he established *La Alianza Federal de las Mercedes* in 1963. The *Alianza*'s goal was to take back the lost land grants by direct action. These Chicanos occupied national forest land, raided the Rio Arriba County Courthouse, and marched on Santa Fe. Tijerina became a national spokesperson for the Chicano movement but his career was shattered when he was convicted of destroying U.S. Forest Service signs and sentenced to three years in the federal penitentiary.

Rudolfo Anaya, New Mexico's native son, was very aware of all the players, the forces, passions, and resentments in the Southwest's tortured history as he worked on *Bless Me, Ultima*. The Chicanos, like Antonio, must decide what to keep and what to let fall away.

## ABOUT RUDOLFO ANAYA

Rudolfo Anaya was born in a place very much like the one he brings to life in the *Bless Me, Ultima*—Pastura, New Mexico—and his parents were very much like Antonio's parents—his mother from a farming family and his father a *vaquero*/cowboy. It was a second marriage for both parents and Anaya was the fifth in a family of seven, with two half-brothers and four sisters. He was delivered by a *curandera*/midwife much like Ultima. Anaya says that such a woman, elderly and wearing a black dress, appeared to him late one night as he worked on his writing, directing him to include her in the novel and name it after her. Once he followed her directions, the novel came together for Anaya. This did not make it any easier to find a publisher, however. He made the rounds for several years and presented the novel to all the mainstream publishing houses with no luck. Publishers were put off by the indiscriminate use of the Spanish language and by the subject matter; they didn't believe a story about Chicanos in New Mexico would have a market outside of that state.

At one point during his infancy, Anaya tells of his mother placing him on the floor surrounded by objects of different professions, for example, a saddle and a guitar. When Rudolfo went straight for the pen and paper, it was evident that his destiny would be a scholarly one. At about this time, the family moved to Santa Rosa where he had a happy, carefree childhood speaking Spanish at home and learning English at school, just like Antonio.

The family, like many others at the time, moved twice during his growing-up years seeking economic stability. Most of the villages in northern New Mexico emptied out after the end of World War II "(in 1940) the majority barely survived by irrigating their one- to four-acre floodplain tracts and by dry farming portions of the homesteaded mesa tracts. (. . .) Gradually, however, villagers gravitated to the cities as men obtained work" (Nostrand 175).

The Anayas settled in Albuquerque when Rudolfo was in eighth grade. His second novel, *Heart of Aztlan*, explores the *choque*/shock he experienced moving from the simple rural childhood to the complex challenges of urban adolescence. When Anaya was 16, he suffered a diving accident and spent that summer in a cast, sharing a hospital room with polio victims. That experience is at the heart of his third novel, *Tortuga* (in Spanish, *tortuga* means turtle, an apt image evoked by the young man wrapped in a cast/shell), which rounds out the trilogy begun with *Bless Me, Ultima*. The mystical and spiritual themes Anaya introduced in *Bless Me, Ultima* appear in *Tortuga* and continue to inhabit a central place in Anaya's universe. Although Anaya takes on political themes such as inequality and discrimination in *Heart of Aztlan*, he has always been most concerned with the Chicano character, the soul of Aztlan.

Rudolfo Anaya began his post-secondary career at business school intending to be an accountant. What a mistake that would have been! A mundane, materialistic profession for this sensitive, scholarly artist. Thankfully, he soon answered his true calling and transferred to the University of New Mexico to earn his BA in English and American literature in 1963. After graduation, he embarked on a long career as an educator, began work on *Bless Me, Ultima*, and on two master's degrees—in English and in Guidance and Counseling. After *Bless Me, Ultima*'s success, Anaya joined the faculty of the University of New Mexico in the English department where he taught, educated, and mentored generations of youth until his retirement in 1993.

It took Rudolfo Anaya many years, false starts, and at least one ghostly visitation to complete *Bless Me, Ultima*. During the fruitless search for a publisher after he had just about given up hope, he came across an ad calling for submissions to the literary journal *El Grito*. Students and professors founded this journal at the University of California, Berkeley, in 1967 in order to provide a place for Chicano writers to be published and validated. A few years later, they established the Quinto Sol Prize to recognize the best fiction written by Mexican American authors. *Bless Me, Ultima* won that prize the second time it was awarded[2] and was published by Editorial Quinto Sol in 1972.

Rudolfo Anaya has since become one of the most revered and respected Chicano authors. He has published in a variety of genres, including children's books, plays, poetry, travel writing, and notably, a quartet of detective novels written in the *noir* style. These novels—*Jemez Spring, Shaman Winter, Rio Grande Fall, Zia Summer*—feature detective Sonny Baca, fictional descendent of legendary lawman Elfego Baca (even in his genre fiction Anaya invokes Mexican American's contentious history; Baca is famous for surviving the Frisco shootout after he tried to arrest a drunk Anglo cowboy). Many of the battles Sonny fights with his nemesis take place in the spirit realm, which puts the books firmly in that magical, mystical place so familiar to Chicano literature.

This prolific writer continues to publish works that explore the themes dear to his heart, works that delve into the spiritual and mythical essence of the history and culture of his native New Mexico. His latest novel is *Randy Lopez Goes Home* (2011). While he has traveled extensively, he continues to live and write daily in Albuquerque.

## WHY WE READ *BLESS ME, ULTIMA*

Ultima came to stay with us the summer I was almost seven. When she came the beauty of the llano unfolded before my eyes, and the gurgling waters of the river sang to the hum of the turning earth. The magical time of childhood stood still, and the pulse of the living earth pressed its mystery into my living blood. She took my hand, and the silent, magic powers she possessed made beauty from the raw, sun-baked llano, the green river valley, and the blue bowl which was the white sun's home. My bare feet felt the throbbing earth and my body trembled with excitement. Time stood still, and it shared with me all that had been, and all that was to come. (1)

From this first powerfully evocative paragraph, Rudolfo Anaya brings to vivid life a time and place that are integral yet strange to the conventional self-image of the United States. *Bless Me, Ultima* follows the classic conventions of the *bildungsroman* or coming-of-age novel, and at its core, it is the boy Antonio's story as he prepares to leave childhood with Ultima's help. But it is much more than that. It is a novel that takes us by the hand and submerges us in Antonio's world—a rural pueblo in the llano of northern New Mexico after World War II—in a visceral way. Anaya succeeds in transcending worn-out stereotypes by creating a piece that feels archetypal in its use of character, language, and setting. All of the characters that people Las Pasturas have their own unique personalities from silly and raucous Horse to Antonio's very different parents to kind and wise Ultima. Yet they are people anyone might recognize from their own youth. Most children have had at least one crazy friend and one wise and kind elder, and aren't most parents at odds with one another, different yet complementary? Anaya's prose in Spanish and English maintains a rhythm throughout the novel that resonates as myth or legend. The earth, the llano, is alive and active, as a character in the novel. The same is true of the animals—Ultima's owl and the golden carp, for example; they are mysterious, and they have depth. While *llano* translates in English as prairie or plains, Anaya's description above does more justice to the term. The northern New Mexico landscape is not the endless rippling prairie of the Midwest but a llano bounded by mountains and forests.

Anaya's portrayal of Las Pasturas, New Mexico, depicts a place that most U.S. Americans are unfamiliar with, a place that seems removed and even exotic. Las Pasturas is now part of the national fabric of the U.S. American quilt, thanks to *Bless Me, Ultima*; this, too, is who we are as a people. Before *Bless Me, Ultima*, the Southwestern United States had mostly been portrayed in Western movies and its Mexican American inhabitants as flimsy and offensive Frito Bandito[3] stereotypes. In those days, movie Mexicans were always the bad guys.

*Bless Me, Ultima* presents a three-dimensional, nuanced portrait of New Mexico and New Mexicans. There are farmers, ranchers, mothers, teachers, priests, healers, and patriots in the novel. Several key characters are World War II veterans.[4] The notions of good and bad are not so clear in this novel; conventional types are turned upside down—the witch is the heroine, the town drunk is a hero, and the "bad guy," Tenorio, is somewhat sympathetic, his rage coming as it does from the painful loss of his evil daughters. We learn, along with Antonio, that human beings are complicated—even if they speak Spanish.

The primal rhythms of life and speech in rural New Mexico inhabit Anaya's gorgeous prose providing an effortless way to tune in to the lilt of Spanish and its syntax. Anaya's decision to incorporate Spanish dialogue seamlessly into the narrative was a risky one at the time, and while it almost kept the book from being published, it is an accurate portrayal of the way most Chicanos communicate and one of the reasons they identified so strongly with *Bless Me, Ultima*. "Code-switching" (alternating between two languages or more) in novels is now common practice and even non-Latino writers such as Cormac McCarthy in *All the Pretty Horses*, for example, include Spanish in dialogue and descriptions without translation, trusting the reader to infer meaning from context. Spanish has been spoken in New Mexico since the time of the Columbian Exchange/ La Conquista; this is another way that the novel alludes to the Chicanos'/ Mexican Americans' long history in this country. Hateful anti-immigrant legislation and other rhetoric that vilify Mexican and other immigrants from Latin America conveniently forget that Mexican American families in the Southwest can trace their roots back longer than many more recent arrivals from Europe.

Since *Bless Me, Ultima*'s publication in 1972, it has been a mainstay on high school reading lists. Included on the National Endowment of the Arts list of classic novels, it was lauded in 2008 as one of the most significant, representative, transcendent Chicano novels of all time. It also has the dubious distinction of appearing consistently on the American Library Association's list of most banned or challenged books largely due to Anaya's depiction of Ultima as a *curandera*/healing woman who uses witchcraft or magic.

Most recently, *Bless Me, Ultima* and other titles were boxed up and removed from the classroom straight away—while the students were sitting in class—in the infamous sacking of Arizona classrooms by the Tucson Unified School District because the Arizona legislature had determined that the books were part of the Mexican American studies program and "Promote[d] resentment toward [a] race or class . . . and . . . advocate[d] ethnic solidarity instead of being individuals." Since none of the other ethnic studies programs were affected, the Hispanic community felt especially singled out and targeted for this egregious affront. The incident inspired a cheeky countermovement by Tejano Tony Díaz, "El Librotraficante" (libro = book; traficante = smuggler), who determined to "smuggle" the banned books back into Arizona from Texas as dangerous and illicit substances. *Bless Me, Ultima* holds an honored place in the trunk of Librotraficante's lowrider as Anaya's tale of a young boy growing up in New Mexico continues to resonate with *los vatos*.

While *Bless Me, Ultima* is not a "political" or "polemical" novel, nor Anaya an overtly "political" writer, the book became a touchstone for Chicano culture that responded to the shared rhythms of an ancient land

and culture. But Chicanos are not the only ones who have been moved by Antonio's story. Readers continue to visit and embrace that ancient land and culture, that strange place made familiar by Anaya's deft storytelling. Finally, Ultima's last words are uplifting encouragement for anyone anywhere—"love life and have the strength to live."

## HISTORICAL EXPLORATIONS

The *llano*, the land, the earth, and throbbing life thrum a primal rhythm throughout *Bless Me, Ultima*. The "llano"—that distinctive topography of the land in northern New Mexico—functions like a character in the novel, a presence with a history and personality. The history of the land in the Southwest represented a grievous injustice to the militants in the Chicano movement. Righting those wrongs and using the recuperated ancestral lands as the home and economic base for a Chicano nation were included as goals for the Chicano movement outlined in the *Plan Espiritual De Aztlán*. In March 1969 at the Chicano Youth Conference in Denver, the youth crafted "El Plan Espiritual De Aztlán," and the poet Alurista penned the preamble claiming the mythic Aztec homeland Aztlán as their heritage. The *Plan* outlined the Chicano vision for their future as a people and as a nation. New Mexico's native son Rudolfo Anaya believes this to be the most significant and transcendent moment of the Chicano movement. He sees this *Plan* as more significant to the Chicano community than even the Treaty of Guadalupe Hidalgo. For him, when the Youth Conference presented "El Plan Espiritual De Aztlán" to the world proclaiming that the movement embraced its Indo-Hispano heritage along with its sacred ties to the land, it gave the movement the potential to move beyond the "limitations of ethnicity to create a world without borders" (Anaya 129).

For Anaya, "Chicano" is

> a particular group under that Hispanic umbrella. More specifically, it means the Mexican-American group and those of us who believed in the Chicano movement and worked in it and created some of our early works in it, made a commitment to the image which the word "Chicano" seems to define. And that image has to do with our commitment to understanding ourselves not only as Hispanic—as people of Spanish and Mexican origins—but as people who also share in the Native American origin and the Native American heritage. Our history is part Indian. (Vasallo, *Conversations* 99)

The youth proclaimed in the *Plan Espiritual* that being a Chicano meant making a commitment, an active claiming of that identity. The Indo-Hispano people are known as *mestizo* in "Old" Mexico where the classic understanding is that the *mestizo* is the offspring of a Spanish conquistador father and the Aztec or indigenous mother who had been conquered and raped. In *Bless Me, Ultima*, Ultima herself embodies the history, tradition, and culture of the llano that stretches all the way back to the times before the Spanish conquest. Anaya invokes both sides (Indo and Hispano) as the wise *curandera*/medicine woman/healer makes use of traditional knowledge: "She spoke to me of the common herbs and medicines we shared with the Indians of the Rio del Norte. She spoke of the ancient medicines of other tribes, the Aztecas, Mayas, and even of those in the old, old country, the Moors" (45).

Ultima's ancient knowledge links her to the origin story of the Aztecs who came to settle and thrive in Tenochtitlan/Mexico City after a long journey from their native land of Aztlán, located in a mystical "northern" desert. Their gods instructed them to search for an eagle on a cactus devouring a serpent. They found that eagle and cactus in the swampy Valley of Mexico and they proceeded to build an improbable empire by overcoming their outcast status and adverse geography. The eagle on the cactus devouring the snake is the iconic image on the Mexican flag and is ubiquitous in Chicano popular art. Aztec imagery and symbolism became integral to the Chicano movement's self-image, and groups from the Chicano literary and artistic world employed terminology and images from the Aztec cultural tradition. The Quinto Sol prize that recognized the best in Chicano literature won by Anaya in 1971 is a case in point. In Aztec mythology, "Quinto Sol" (sol = sun) refers to the present age preceded by four ages or "suns" of creation and destruction. Gonzo journalist Hunter S. Thompson recognized Aztlán as the Chicano homeland in the first piece he wrote for *Rolling Stone* magazine in 1971, "Strange Rumblings in Aztlán."

Claiming the Aztec legacy brought Chicanos a newfound dignity after being scorned on both sides of the border for being *ni de aquí ni de allá*. Author of what is considered the first Chicano novel, *Pocho*, Jose Antonio Villarreal portrayed this experience as suffered by his protagonist, the "pocho" of the title. He is a young Mexican immigrant, growing up in the United States who faces the situation that was so familiar to Chicanos: rejected by Mexicans because he acts too "American" and despised by U.S. Americans for being Mexican.

An early portrayal of the Chicano experience appeared in 1928 published in weekly installments in Los Angeles's Spanish language newspaper *El heraldo de México* titled *Las aventuras de Don Chipote* (The Adventures of Don Chipote) by Daniel Venegas. The novel, a kind of Mexican parody of Don Quixote, tells of Don Chipote and his faithful dog Sufrelambre (Skinnenbones) and their travails in Gringolandia—the United States—with broad humor and earthy language. Don Chipote and Sufrelambre end up returning to Mexico; the story is a morality tale for would-be immigrants: "It was a memory that would not let him forget the troubles that Chicanos experience when leaving their fatherland, made starry-eyed by the yarns spun by those who go to the United States, as they say, to strike it rich" (Venegas 160). The youth participating in the Chicano movement took ownership of the term and transformed it into a badge of solidarity, of dignity, and of pride.

In the case of *Bless Me, Ultima*, like most New Mexicans, almost all of the characters in the novel are Chicano, but, unlike the protagonists above, they are not immigrants. They are the Chicanos' link to Aztlán. In "El Plan Espiritual De Aztlán," the Chicano youth also called themselves *mestizo*, bronze race and people of the sun in a way that emphasized their claim to pre-Hispanic roots. This mixed status in a country obsessed with classification has made *raza* (race) a concept central to the Chicano movement and the phrase *¡Viva la raza!* has been shouted at every march and protest. The National Council of La Raza is the largest national Hispanic civil rights and advocacy organization in the United States that was founded during the Civil Rights and Chicano movement of the 1960s. A political party, La Raza Unida Party (The Raza United), mobilized Chicanos nationally. The National Council of La Raza, on the other hand, has expanded to embrace all Latino groups while becoming a significant and trusted voice for Chicanos. Although the word *raza* is sometimes misunderstood as "racist," the concept seeks to transcend and embrace all races; the *raza de bronce* would rise to an exceptional level by integrating the best qualities of all races.

This *mestizo*/mixed *raza* heritage is explored at length in *I Am Joaquin* by Corky Gonzales. In the epic poem, the narrator Joaquin evokes the famous "outlaw" Joaquin Murieta who has become a legend.[5] Gonzales weaves together themes, motifs, and origin stories for a brilliant exposition of the twin contradictory strands (Indo and Hispano) of Chicano heritage. Rodolfo "Corky" Gonzales was one of the leaders at the Denver Youth Conference, and presented "El Plan Espiritual De Aztlán" at that event. Just as *Bless Me, Ultima* continues to be read, so does *I Am Joaquin*, which Dreamers (undocumented youth raised in the United States) continue to declaim and proclaim.

By Antonio's time, the Aztecs had long been conquered by the Spanish. Tony's struggle with faith is one of the main themes of the book, recreating the clash of indigenous faith traditions against the powerful institution of the Catholic Church from the time of the Colombian Exchange. Antonio as a thoughtful, questing, sensitive child feels the visceral pull of the primal in the form of the golden carp:

> He was beautiful; he was truly a god. The white sun reflected off his bright orange scales and the glistening glorious light blinded us and filled us with the rapture true beauty brings. Seeing him made questions and worries evaporate, and I remained transfixed, caught and caressed by the essential elements of sky and earth and water. The sun warmed us with its life-giving power, and up in the sky a white moon smiled on us. (251–252)

On the other hand, the strict and empty rituals of the Catholic Church alienate him: "The water was icy. The church was cold and musty. . .Florence's punishment for being late was to stand in the middle of the aisle with his arms outspread. . . holding the weight of his arms which would become numb like lead before catechism was over" (209).

Antonio does venerate the warm, loving, and accepting Virgin of Guadalupe:

> We all knew the story of how the Virgin had presented herself to the little Indian boy in Mexico and about the miracles she had wrought. My mother said the Virgin was the saint of our land, and although there were many other good saints, I loved none as dearly as the Virgin (. . .) God was not always forgiving. He made laws to follow and if you broke them you were punished. The Virgin always forgave. . . The Virgin was full of a quiet, peaceful love. (47)

The Virgin of Guadalupe is another Chicano icon; Cesar Chavez prominently used her image on banners and altars during the farmworkers' long struggle. The Spaniards built the great Basilica of Guadalupe, one of the most important and visited shrines in the Americas at the site where the Virgin presented herself to Juan Diego. That site is thought to have been the place used by the Aztecs to worship their Mother goddess, Tonantzin. One of the Spaniards' strategies for conversion was to blend Catholic saints with "similar" deities from the culture they were converting/conquering; the Indians could covertly continue to venerate their gods. The Virgin of Guadalupe/Tonantzin is an example of the blending of cultures, *sincretismo*/syncretism; she is Indo-Hispano, like the *mestizo*, and is revered throughout Latin America and in the Southwestern United States.

An area that did not lend itself to syncretism was the difference in land usage between Anglos and New Mexicans after the U.S.–Mexican

War of 1848. Antonio addresses this difference by describing at length the llano's history, his family's place in that history, and its strong ties to the llano. In Las Pasturas, Tony's family feels the anguish of the Anglo invasion when their way of life had been marginalized and devalued. At the beginning of *Bless Me, Ultima*, he presents a synopsis of New Mexico's history and Anaya returns to that history throughout the novel as he impresses its trajectory upon the reader:

> He spoke in Spanish and the village he mentioned was his home. My father had been a vaquero all his life, a calling as ancient as the coming of the Spaniard to Nuevo Méjico. Even after the big rancheros and the tejanos came and fenced the beautiful llano, he and those like him continued to work there, I guess because only in that wide expanse of land and sky could they feel the freedom their spirits needed. (2)

And later:

> "Long ago," (Ultima) would smile, "long before you were a dream, long before the train came to Las Pasturas, before the Lunas came to their valley, before the great Coronado built his bridge-" Then her voice would trail off and my thoughts would be lost in the labyrinth of a time and history I did not know. (43)

Here Tony's mother speaks of the land grant or "charter" during an argument with his father:

> You leave my brothers out of this! They are honorable men. They have always treated you with respect. They were the first colonizers of the Llano Estacado. It was the Lunas who carried the charter from the Mexican government to settle the valley. That took courage. (55)

And from his father's point of view:

> But always the talk would return to stories of the old days in Las Pasturas. Always the talk turned to life on the llano. The first pioneers were sheepherders. Then they imported herds of cattle from Mexico and became vaqueros. They became horsemen, caballeros, men whose daily life was wrapped up in the ritual of horsemanship. They were the first cowboys in a wild and desolate land which they took from the Indians.
>
> Then the railroad came. The barbed wire came. The songs, the corridos became sad, and the meeting of the people from Texas with my forefathers was full of blood, murder, and tragedy. The people became uprooted. They looked around one day and found themselves closed in. The freedom of land and sky they had known was gone. (130–131)

In this passage, Ultima presents the indigenous and spiritual roots of the llano:

> "A long time ago," she began, "the llano of the Agua Negra was the land of the Comanche Indians. Then the comancheros came, then the Mexican with his flocks—many years ago three Comanche Indians raided the flocks of one man, and this man was the grandfather of Tellez. Tellez gathered the other Mexicans around him and they hanged the three Indians. They left the bodies strung on a tree; they did not bury them according to their custom. Consequently, the three souls were left to wander on that ranch. The brujas who laid the curse knew this, so instead of placing the curse on a member of the family and taking the chance of getting caught, they simply awakened the ghosts of the three Indians and forced them to do the wrong. The three tortured spirits are not to blame, they are manipulated by brujas."

Anaya himself knew firsthand about the land grants' contentious history. He inherited three shares of stock in the Atrisco Land Grant, which lies on the West mesa of Albuquerque, some 49,000 acres. Anaya vehemently protested, unsuccessfully, the sale of the grant to investors for development. He contended that:

> The land was not given to us by our ancestors to sell. The land was to be passed down to future generations to be used for the social good of the community (. . .) The land belonged to the community, it was cared for, it was the mother earth which nurtured us. It provided firewood, grass, and water for grazing animals. Over the centuries the people developed a spiritual attachment to the land. (Anaya 131–132)

*Bless Me, Ultima* powerfully invokes the history of the land in the Southwest so drastically affected by the Treaty of Guadalupe Hidalgo. The treaty spells out the conditions of surrender that ceded over half of Mexican territory to the United States, a seminal moment for all Chicanos. The treaty was regarded in a similar way as the treaties made with the Native American tribes, however, and Mexicans were likewise regarded as racially inferior, undeserving of fair treatment.

Before the ink was dry on the Treaty of Guadalupe Hidalgo, territorial governors and their cronies colluded to bilk New Mexicans out of their birthright. Thomas Catron, who arrived in New Mexico in the late 1860s, was one of the people to benefit greatly; he was much later linked to one of the worst known cases of corruption in the United States, the Teapot Dome Scandal of the early 1920s. All in all, New Mexicans were "outmaneuvered" (Norstrand) by Anglos and lost some 20 million acres.

This "outmaneuvering" consisted of shenanigans like territorial Gov. Pile (1869–1871) burning and destroying paper deeds as waste paper in Santa Fe (the Mexican copies mysteriously burned up in a fire in Guadalajara around the same time) and included outright terror.

> From 1848 to 1928, mobs murdered thousands of Mexicans. . . Some of these cases did appear in press accounts, when reporters depicted them as violent public spectacles (. . .) While there were similarities between the lynchings of blacks and Mexicans, there were also clear differences. One was that local authorities and deputized citizens played particularly conspicuous roles in mob violence against Mexicans.
> (William D. Carrigan and Clive Webb, *New York Times*, February 20, 2015, Vol. 164 Issue 56783, A27)

Around 1887, one of the early organized efforts at self-defense came in the form of a clandestine group called *Las gorras blancas* (The White Caps). These men went out under cover of night to tear down fences so that people could get access to grazing land for their livestock. They advocated for fair treatment and the just resolution of land grant claims. Their leader, Juan José Herrera, was a veteran of the Civil War and later helped to create the first all-Hispano political party, *El Partido del Pueblo* (The Party of the People). Like other men who suffered injustice in the 19th century and fought back, he was labeled an outlaw. Other such men, like Joaquín Murieta in California and Juan Nepomuceno Cortina in Texas, were hunted down and executed.

In the 20th century, a different kind of outlaw, Reies Lopez Tijerina, also fought for justice for Chicanos and spent a lot of time in jail for it. He began life on the Texas-Mexico border, picking cotton as a child, and later followed the crops as a migrant worker. Recruited by an Assembly of God evangelist preacher, he joined that church and became an itinerant minister. While doing missionary work in Mexico, he was inspired by the populist rhetoric of the Mexican revolution and returned to the United States to establish a cooperative community in Arizona. He learned about the land grant situation and determined to see justice done. He organized the land grant families into a group called La Alianza Federal de Mercedes (The Federal Land Grant Alliance) and traveled to Mexico City to research the land grants. He then pursued the issue in the courts and through actions such as citizens' arrests of prominent figures, lawsuits, and marches—actions that many times got him, his family members, and friends arrested. By the time he was finally released from his last stint in prison, his spirit was broken.

About the time that Tijerina was establishing his Village of Peace Co-op in Arizona, Cleofas Jaramillo's memoir *Romance of a Little Village Girl* was published in 1955. Cleofas Jaramillo was born in New Mexico territory in 1878 into the privileged class. She had a sheltered childhood, attending convent school where she learned English. Her memoir paints an idyllic picture of growing up in a village near Taos in the same region where Anaya spent his childhood and set *Bless Me, Ultima*. Mrs. Jaramillo spent her later years defending and working to preserve the New Mexican native culture. Besides *Romance*, she published a cookbook and a collection of the traditional tales she learned from her mother. Mrs. Jaramillo's husband, Venceslao Jaramillo, was a delegate to the New Mexico state constitutional convention in 1912 and served as state senator. His death at an early age forced Cleofas Jaramillo to confront the limitations of her privileged upbringing and salvage something of her husband's property in order to raise her daughter.

Ultima, Antonio, his family, his friends, and his neighbors play out a human tale in *Bless Me, Ultima* about a child growing up and confronting the large questions of existence in a unique place. The Chicano spirit and its history, roots and destiny flow through the text and bring us to examine the heart and soul of the Southwest. When Chicanos protest injustice and abuse and advocate for positive change for their community, *Bless Me, Ultima* demonstrates that the resentments run deep for a pueblo/people that has survived multiple invasions. The Chicanos endure with a spirit like Antonio's who, after her death, is charged with Ultima's work of helping others, of carrying on the ancient legacy, and of striving toward harmony.

## DOCUMENTING *BLESS ME, ULTIMA*

### Aztlán: The Aztec Legacy

*Bless Me, Ultima* takes place far north of Mexico City but squarely in the heart of what Chicanos consider Aztlán—the Aztec's mysterious land of origin—in the Southwestern United States where Americans of Mexican descent have resided since the times of the Spanish conquistadors. The first document is taken from Mexican anthropologist Miguel León Portillo seminal work *The Broken Spears: The Aztec Account of the Conquest of Mexico*, first published in English in 1962.[6] The Chicanos recognized their own history in this book, seeing themselves as doubly conquered—first by the Spanish and then by the Anglo in 1848. *The Fall of Tenochtitlan* expresses the Aztecs' deep sadness and despair as they saw their city and their way of life destroyed by the conquistadors.

On the occasion of the 500th anniversary year of Columbus's arrival in the New World, internationally renowned Mexican author Carlos Fuentes published *The Buried Mirror*, a biography of Spanish culture and its legacy in the Americas. His interpretation of one of the Aztec elegies highlights the Aztec despair and the conquistadors' duplicity and culpability in the second document.

The third document, "El Plan Espiritual De Aztlán," declared young Chicanos' identification with their Aztec heritage and demands for liberation. Presented at the youth moratorium in Denver in 1969, the youth proposed Aztlán as the site for a reborn Chicano nation.

# From "Elegies on the Fall of the City" in *Broken Spears*, 1523
## The Fall of Tenochtitlan

Our cries of grief rise up
and our tears rain down,
for Tlatelolco is lost.
The Aztecs are fleeing across the lake;
they are running away like women.
How can we save our homes, my people?
The Aztecs are deserting the city:
the city is in flames, and all
is darkness and destruction.
Motelchiuhtzin the Huiznahuacatl,
Tlacotzin the Tlailotlacatl,
Oquitzin the Tlacatecuhtli
are greeted with tears.
Weep, my people:
know that with these disasters
we have lost the Mexican nation.
The water has turned bitter,
our food is bitter!
These are the acts of the Giver of Life.

*Source:* Miguel León Portillo, ed. *The Broken Spears: The Aztec Account of the Conquest of Mexico* (Boston: Beacon Press, 1962), 145–149.

# From *The Buried Mirror*, 1992

All of the Indian societies of the Americas, whatever their political failings, were young, creative civilizations. The Spanish conquest arrested them, stunted their growth, and left them with a legacy of sadness, which one hears in the "vision of the defeated" as the compiler of their writings, Miguel Leon-Portilla, calls them. This sadness was sung by the ragged poets of the defeated Indian world.

Where shall we go now, oh my friends?
The smoke is rising, the fog is spreading.
Cry, my friends.
The waters are red.
Cry, oh cry, for we have lost the Aztec nation.

The time of the fifth sun was at an end.
As for the conquerors, they could echo these words, for what they had at first admired, they had now destroyed.

*Source:* Excerpts from *The Buried Mirror* by Carlos Fuentes (New York: Houghton Mifflin Co., 1992), 116–117. Copyright © 1992 by Carlos Fuentes. Reprinted by permission of Houghton Mifflin Harcourt Publishing Company. All rights reserved.

# From *El Plan Espiritual De Aztlán*, 1969

## Introduction

In the spirit of a new people that is conscious not only of its proud histori-cal heritage, but also of the brutal "Gringo" invasion of our territories, we, the Chicano inhabitants and civilizers of the Northern land of Aztlán, from whence came our forefathers, reclaiming the land of their birth and conse-crating the determination of our people of the sun, declare that the call of our blood is our power, our response and our inevitable destiny.

We are free and sovereign to determine those tasks which are justly called for by our house, the sweat of our brows and by our hearts. Aztlán belongs to those that plant the seeds, water the land and gather the crops, and not to foreign Europeans. We do not recognize capricious frontiers on the Bronze Continent.

Brotherhood unites us, and love of our brothers makes us a people whose time has come and who struggle against the foreign "Gabacho" who exploits our riches and destroys our culture. With our hearts in our hands and our hands in the soil, we declare the independence of our Mestizo nation, a Bronze people with a Bronze culture. Before the world, before all of North America, before our brothers in the Bronze continent, We are a Nation of free pueblos, we are Aztlán.

—Alurista, March 1969

### The Program of El Plan De Aztlán

1. "El Plan Espiritual De Aztlán" sets the theme that the Chicanos (La Raza de Bronze) must use their nationalism as the key or

common denominator for mass mobilization and organization. Once we are committed to the idea and philosophy of El Plan De Aztlán, we can only conclude that social, economic, cultural and political independence is the only road to total liberation from oppression, exploitation and racism. Our struggle then must be the control of our Barrios, campos, pueblos, lands, our economy, our culture and our political life. El Plan commits all levels of Chicano society—the barrio, the campo, the rancho, the writer, the teacher, the worker, the professional—to La Causa.

## I. Punto Primero—Nationalism

Nationalism as the key to organization transcends all religious, political, class and economic factions or boundaries. Nationalism is the common denominator that all members of La Raza can agree on.

## II. Punto Segundo—Organizational Goals

1.  Unity in thought of our people concerning the barrios, the land, the poor, the middle class, the professional is committed to liberation of La Raza.
2.  Economy: economic control of our lives and our communities can only come about by driving the exploiter out of our communities, our pueblos, and our lands and by controlling and developing our own talents, sweat and resources. Cultural background and values which ignore materialism and embrace humanism will lend to the act of co-operative buying and distribution of resources and production to sustain an economic base for healthy growth and development. Lands rightfully ours will be fought for and defended. Land and realty ownership will be acquired by the community for the people's welfare. Economic ties of responsibility must be secured by nationalism and the Chicano defense units.
3.  Education must be relative to our people, i.e., history, culture, bilingual education, contributions, etc. Community control of our schools, our teachers, our administrators, our counselors and our programs.
4.  Institutions shall serve our people by providing the service necessary for a full life and their welfare on the basis of restitution, not handouts or beggar's crumbs. Restitution for past economic slavery, political exploitation, ethnic, cultural and psychological destruction and denial of civil and human rights. Institutions in our community

which do not serve the people have no place in the community. The institutions belong to the people.

5.  Self Defense of the community must rely on the combined strength of the people. The front line defense will come from the barrios, the campos, the pueblos, and the ranchitos. Their involvement as protectors of their people will be given respect and dignity. They in turn offer their responsibility and their lives for their people. Those who place themselves on the front for their people do so out of love and carnalismo. Those institutions which are fattened by our brothers to provide employment and political pork barrels for the gringo will do so only by acts of liberation and La Causa. For the very young there will no longer be acts of juvenile delinquency, but revolutionary acts.

6.  Cultural values of our people strengthen our identity and the moral backbone of the movement. Our culture unites and educates the family of La Raza toward liberation with one heart and one mind. We must insure that our writers, poets, musicians and artists produce literature and art that is appealing to our people and relates to our revolutionary culture. Our cultural values of life, family, and home will serve as a powerful weapon to defeat the gringo dollar value system and encourage the process of love and brotherhood.

7.  Political liberation can only come through an independent action on our part, since the two party system is the same animal with two heads that feeds from the same trough. Where we are a majority we will control; where we are a minority, we will represent a pressure group; Nationally, we will represent one party, La Familia de La Raza.

*III.  Punto Tercero—Action*

1.  Awareness and distribution of El Plan Espiritual De Aztlan. Presented at every meeting, demonstration, confrontation, court house, institution, administration, church, school, building, car and every place of human existence.

2.  September 16th. On the birthdate of Mexican Independence, a national walk-out by all Chicanos of all colleges and schools to be sustained until the complete revision of the educational system; its policy makers, administration, its curriculum and its personnel to meet the needs of the community.

3.  Self defense against the occupying forces of the oppressors at every shcool [sic], every available man, woman and child.

4. Community nationalization and organization of all Chicanos regarding El Plan Espiritual De Aztlán.
5. Economic programs to drive the exploiter out of our communities and a welding of our peoples combined resources to control their own production through co-operative efforts.
6. Creation of an independent local, regional and national political party.

*Liberation*

A nation, autonomously free, culturally, socially, economically and politically, will make its own decisions on the usage of our lands, the taxation of our goods, the utilization of our bodies for war, the determination of justice (reward and punishment) and the profit of our sweat.

**El Plan Espiritutal [*sic*] De Aztlán
is the Plan of Liberation!**

Source: El Plan Espiritual De Aztlán. Adopted at the First National Chicano Liberation Youth Conference in Denver, Colorado, March 1969. Full text available at: http://www. umich.edu/~mechaum/Aztlan.html. Retrieved 6/26/2015.

**Ethnicity and Identity: *La Raza***

In *Bless Me, Ultima*, Anaya stresses the Indo-Hispano ethnicity of the characters. This mestizo identity was crucial to the Chicano movement. "El Plan Espiritual De Aztlán" cited earlier names Chicanos as *La Raza de Bronze*, which is shortened to *La Raza* and calls for the "liberation of La Raza."

The concept of *La Raza* can be traced to José Vasconcelos's groundbreaking work, "La Raza Cósmica"/The Cosmic Race. The Mexican Revolution of 1910 brought with it the rejection of European cultural influence and foreign interference. Mexican intellectuals, like Vasconcelos, understood that Mexico needed to embrace its *mestizo*/mixed race heritage in order to fulfill its destiny as a sovereign nation. The first document is an excerpt from *The Cosmic Race*, which later inspired Chicanos to interpret their Indo-Hispanic/*mestizo* heritage as *La Raza*.

In the second document, Carlos Fuentes echoes this sentiment in his analysis of the Spanish legacy in the Americas. The Spanish American aleph alludes to the short story by Jorge Luis Borges (the aleph as a point that contains all other points) and emphasizes that "La Raza Cósmica" encompasses all of the Americas.

Chicano leader Corky Gonzales helped to organize the Youth Moratorium in Denver. In the third document, an excerpt from his classic and
beloved poem, *I Am Joaquin*, he lyrically traces Chicanos' *mestizo* heritage. U.S. poet laureate Juan Felipe Herrera has called this poem "our
(the Chicanos') collective song that arrived like thunder crashing from the
heavens."

## From "The Cosmic Race," 1925

The purpose of the new and ancient continent is much more important. Its
predestination obeys the design of constituting the cradle of a fifth race
into which all nations will fuse with each other to replace the four races
that have been forging History apart from each other. The dispersion will
come to an end on American soil; unity will be consummated there by the
triumph of fecund love and the improvement of all the human races. In this
fashion, the synthetic race that shall gather all the treasures of History in
order to give expression to universal desire shall be created.

The so-called Latin peoples, because they have been more faithful to
their divine mission in America, are the ones called upon to consummate
this mission. Such fidelity to the occult design is the guarantee of our
triumph.

(. . .)

How different the sounds of the Ibero-American development (from
Anglo-Saxon North American development)! They resemble the profound
scherzo of a deep and infinite symphony: (. . .) So many races that have
come and others that will come. In this manner, a sensitive and ample
heart will be taking shape within us; a heart that embraces and contains
everything and is moved with sympathy, but, full of vigor, imposes new
laws upon the world. And we foresee something like another head that
will dispose of all angles in order to fulfill the miracle of surpassing the
sphere.

## From *The Buried Mirror*, 1992

What we would see in the Spanish American aleph would be the Indian
sense of sacredness, communality, and the will to survive; the Mediter-
ranean legacy of law, philosophy, and the Christian, Jewish, and Arab

strains making up a multiracial Spain; and the New World's challenge to Spain, the syncretic, baroque continuation of the multicultural and multiracial experience, now including Indian, European, and black African contributions. We would see a struggle for democracy and for revolution, coming all the way from the medieval townships and from the ideas of the European Enlightenment, but meeting our true personal and communal experience in Zapata's villages, on Bolívar's plains, in Tupac Amarú's highlands.

*Source:* Excerpts from *The Buried Mirror* by Carlos Fuentes (New York: Houghton Mifflin Co., 1992), 349. Copyright © 1992 by Carlos Fuentes. Reprinted by permission of Houghton Mifflin Harcourt Publishing Company. All rights reserved.

## From *I Am Joaquin*, 1967

I am Joaquín,
Lost in a world of confusion,
Caught up in the whirl of a
gringo society,
confused by the rules,
scorned by attitudes,
suppressed by manipulation,
and destroyed by modern society.
My fathers
have lost the economic battle
and won
the struggle of cultural survival.

And now!
I must choose
        between
the paradox of
victory of the spirit,
despite physical hunger
        or
to exist in the grasp
of American social neurosis,
sterilization of the soul

and a full stomach.

Yes.
I have come a long way to nowhere
unwillingly dragged by that
monstrous, technical,

industrial giant called
       progress
and Anglo success. . .

I look at myself.
I watch my brothers.
        I shed tears of sorrow.
                  I sow seeds of hate.
        I withdraw to the safety within the
circle of life-


## MY OWN PEOPLE

I am Cuauhtémoc,
proud and noble,
leader of men,
king of an empire
civilized beyond the dreams
of the gachupín Cortés,
who also is the blood,
the image of myself.
I am the Maya prince.
I am Nezahualcoyotl,
great leader of the Chichimecas.
I am the sword and flame of Cortés,
        the despot.
        and
I am the eagle and serpent of
        the Aztec civilization.

I owned the land as far as the eye
could see under the crown of Spain,
and I toiled on my earth
and gave my Indian sweat and blood
for the Spanish master
who ruled with tyranny over man and
beast and all that he could trample.
                       but. . .


## THE GROUND WAS MINE

I was both tyrant and slave.

*Source: I Am Joaquin* by Rodolfo "Corky" Gonzales from Ilan Stavans, ed. *The Norton Anthology of Latino Literature* (New York: W. W. Norton, 2011), 788–789. Copyright © 1967 Rodolfo "Corky" Gonzales.

# Land and Loss: The Travesty of the Treaty of Guadalupe Hidalgo

The first document presents Articles VIII and IX from the Treaty of Guadalupe Hidalgo in place to protect the interests and patrimony of erstwhile Mexican citizens residing in U.S. territory after the U.S.–Mexican War. Mexican residents in New Mexico territory formed alliances to combat abuse and mistreatment in clandestine groups like *Las gorras blancas*. In the second document, the platform of *Las gorras blancas* manifests the Mexicans' determination to defend their families and their interests. The third document is from the transcript of a fiery radio interview given shortly after Martin Luther King Jr.'s assassination. In the interview, Reies Lopez Tijerina explains the injustice that has played out over the history of New Mexico in the case of the land grants. He describes his group (La Alianza Federal de Mercedes) and their struggle to right those wrongs and finishes with an explanation of the Chicano's *mestizo*/indo-hispano identity.

The fourth document is the memoir of Cleofas Jaramillo who was born into a well-to-do family in New Mexico territory near Rudolfo Anaya's hometown of Pasturas and married a senator who helped fashion the state's constitution. The somewhat bucolic portrayal by a daughter of the privileged class is laced with subtle resentment but brimming with pride about New Mexico's Spanish heritage reminding us once again that the Spanish settled New Mexico long before the English put down roots on the East Coast. The memoir is a pretty tale and although Mrs. Jaramillo tactfully declines to denounce the wrongs she must have suffered, the text contains traces of subtle indignation and evidence of the chaotic nature of politics in New Mexico before statehood.

# From The Treaty of Guadalupe Hidalgo, 1848

The United States of America and the United Mexican States, animated by a sincere desire to put an end to the calamities of the war which unhappily exists between the two republics, and to establish upon a solid basis relations of peace and friendship, which shall confer reciprocal benefits upon the citizens of both, and assure the concord, harmony, and mutual confidence wherein the two people should live, as good neighbors, have for that purpose appointed their respective plenipotentiaries. . .

### *Article VIII*

Mexicans now established in territories previously belonging to Mexico, and which remain for the future within the limits of the United States, as defined by the present treaty, shall be free to continue where they now reside, or to remove at any time to the Mexican republic, retaining the property which they possess in the said territories, or disposing thereof, and removing the proceeds wherever they please, without their being subjected, on this account, to any contribution, tax, or charge whatever.

Those who shall prefer to remain in the said territories, may either retain the title and rights of Mexican citizens, or acquire those of citizens of the United States. But they shall be under the obligation to make their election within one year from the date of exchange of ratifications of this treaty; and those who shall remain in the said territories after the expiration of that year, without having declared their intention to retain the character of Mexicans, shall be considered to have elected to become citizens of the United States.

In the said territories, property of every kind, now belonging to Mexicans not established there, shall be inviolably respected. The present owners, the heirs of these, and all Mexicans who may hereafter acquire said property by contract, shall enjoy with respect to it guaranties equally ample as if the same belonged to citizens of the United States.

### Article IX

Mexicans who, in the territories aforesaid, shall not preserve the character of citizens of the Mexican republic, conformably with what is stipulated in the preceding article, shall be incorporated into the Union of the United States, and be admitted at the proper time . . . to the enjoyment of all the rights of citizens of the United States, according to the principles of the constitution; and in the mean time shall be maintained and protected in the free enjoyment of their liberty and property, and secured in the free exercise of their religion without restriction.

Source: The Treaty of Guadalupe Hidalgo, February 2, 1848. Treaty of Peace, Friendship, Limits, and Settlement with the Republic of Mexico. *Treaties and Conventions between the United States of America and Other Powers Since July 4, 1776* (Washington, DC: Government Printing Office, 1871).

# From *Platform of* Las Gorras Blancas, 1890

*Our Platform*

Not wishing to be misunderstood, we hereby make this our declaration.

Our purpose is to protect the rights and interests of the people in general, especially those of the helpless classes.

We want the Las Vegas Grant settled to the benefit of all concerned, and this we hold is the entire community within the grant.

We want no "land grabbers" or obstructionists of any sort to interfere. We will watch them.

We are not down on lawyers as a class, but the usual knavery and unfair treatment of the people must be stopped.

Our judiciary hereafter must understand that we will sustain it only when "Justice" is its watchword.

The practice of "double-dealing" must cease.

There is a wide difference between New Mexico's "law" and "justice." And justice is God's law, and that we must have at all hazards.

We are down on race issues, and will watch race agitators. We are all human brethren, under the same glorious flag.

We favor irrigation enterprises, but will fight any scheme whose purpose is to monopolize the supply of water courses to the detriment of residents living on lands watered by the same streams.

We favor all enterprises, but object to corrupt methods to further the same.

We do not care how much you get as long as you do it fairly and honestly.

The People are suffering from the effects of partisan "bossism," and these bosses had better quietly hold their peace. The people have been persecuted and hacked about in every which way to satisfy their caprice. If they persist in their usual methods, retribution will be their reward.

We are watching "political informers."

We have no grudge against any person in particular, but we are the enemies of bulldozers and tyrants.

We must have a free ballot and a fair count, and the will of the majority shall be respected.

Intimidation and the "indictment" plan have no further fears for us. If the old system should continue, death would be a relief to our sufferings. And for our rights, our lives are the least we can pledge.

If the fact that we are law-abiding citizens is questioned, come to our homes and see the hunger and desolation we are suffering; and "this" is the result of the deceitful and corrupt methods of "bossism."

Be fair and just and we are with you; do otherwise and take the consequences.

The White Caps, 1,500 Strong and Growing Daily

*Source:* "Platform of Las Gorras Blancas Issued by Juan José Herrera," *Las Vegas Daily Optic* (March 12, 1890).

# From *Tijerina Speaks Out on Martin Luther King's Assassination,* 1968

I would like to state that the people of New Mexico, like the Hopi nation, have never surrendered to the confiscation of the land; have never surrendered to the federal government and to their ideas; . . .which are against the three-hundred-year-old system and way of livelihood in New Mexico. There is a group, there was and there is, called White Caps in the Northern part of New Mexico. As the government builds fences around this common land that belongs to the villages, during the day, the people cut the fences during the night, on and on for the last hundred years. The government has conspired in a thousand ways to destroy the lives, the culture, the language, the property of the people. It has not succeeded in pushing the people out of the northern part of New Mexico.

(. . .) My first step after discovering that they held a true claim and that the treaty did stipulate the protection of such land, and that they did have the title, and the villages had title to this land, I decided to organize and unite the people of the various land grants, which are called pueblos. It is these pueblos who hold the land, not the individuals, not the heirs. The heirs held certain rights through the village, through the pueblo council, or city councils, more popularly called. And in 1963, after due and thorough investigation, I decided to organize the Alianza Federal de Mercedes, Federal Alliance of Land Grants, whose papers and documents were confiscated by the federal government in 1967. . .

(. . .)

It was when we were to hold a meeting, a nationwide meeting, in Coyote, New Mexico. . . the state police believe (d) that there was going to be a shootout, the district attorney . . .decided to pool all his resources and call the chief of police. . .and call all his state militia, state police, block all the roads, and start arresting everybody on the grounds of unlawful assembly. Naturally the people were too strong, too brave to swallow such a stupid accusation and grounds for arrest. They were enraged, they were angry, and in this state of anger, the following day after the mass arrest, they decided to arrest, by themselves, the District Attorney. They were furnished with a warrant of arrest, an official document signed by the *alcalde*, the mayor of San Joaquin. The deputies and the volunteers went to Tierra Amarilla, the next town, to arrest Alfonso Sánchez. It was a plain citizen's arrest.

(. . .)

Interviewer: the original Treaty of Guadalupe did reserve to your people these pueblo lands and certain rights?

(. . .)

. . .the cultural rights, which includes the language: property rights, which includes the mode of, or the way of living, that is concerning the property. See, we held no property individually, but a little home and a little garden. We could not hold over 150 square yards for ourselves. It was the pueblo, the village that held all the land in trust for the villagers. So naturally, the government comes and respects the Indian pueblos, but the Spanish pueblos, it froze them, confiscated the land, took it, converted it into public land or U.S. Forest land under the Department of Agriculture and the Department of the Interior. So, naturally, that was an outright theft. . . (. . .) To start with, the public has not been told that after the treaty was signed, our government took full responsibility as our government to protect our lives and our property. . . . in the year 1870, William A. Pile, governor of the Territory of New Mexico, with the help of the territorial attorney general, who was Thomas B. Catron, the king leader and the king of New Mexico for fifty years, the criminal shrewd person who masterminded the whole plan, took William Pile and Thomas B. Catron, kicked out the archives of Santa Fe-the documents that had been kept there for three hundred years. They were kicked out in the street, according to historians Twitchell and Bancroft. According to newspaper film of that day, an editorial called William Pile, a "Pig Head" for kicking the Spanish archives out into the streets.

I'd like to state that during these years, there was no judicial protection for the land grant titles, for the pueblos, for our property. There was no protection from 1848 to 1891; there was no judicial or tribunal hearings for the adjudication of these titles. It was in the year 1891 when Frank Springer, a friend of Thomas B. Catron and a member of the Santa Fe Ring, asked Congress to establish a political court to adjudicate the titles. It was from 1891 to 1904 that the titles were adjudicated by tribunals of five judges who were all veterans of the Civil War, and veterans of the Confederacy, of the South, who hated the Spanish Americans and the Mexicans. . .

(On "raza")

. . .we are fighting and teaching our people the difference between Mexican-American and Spanish-American and Chicano, La Raza, Hispano, Latino, and. . . all those names. We feel that we are not Spaniards, not Indians, as the history will state and prove; we are a new breed that for the last three hundred years has been multiplying at a very fast rate. . . See, the new breed, according to law and records, is Indio-Hispano (. . .) Hispano means sprinkled with something from Spain, (. . .) We are saying "Hispano" which means a race, a people that is sprinkled with Spanish blood. However, according to Law II, Title 1, Book 6 of the Law of the

Indias. . . we are *indio-hispanos*. That covers the Indian part and the Hispanic part. (311–317)

*Source:* Archive #BB1820 "Reies López Tijerina Interviewed by Elsa Knight
Thompson," April 5, 1968, Pacifica News Archives. To browse their 55,000 recordings,
go to www.PacificaRadioARchives.org.

## From *"In the Royal Village of the Holy Faith,"* *Romance of the Little Village Girl*, 1955

By my fifth year at the Convent School in Taos, I noticed that I was making slow progress in my grades. No exams were held. There were no pro-
motions, only the beginning of a higher reader, an Olendorf, or some other
new book, added to the same grade. I told my father about it and prepara-
tions were made for my entrance at the Loretto Academy, at La Villa Real
de Santa Fe. Autumn's coloring brush had already touched the little valley
turning its summer greenery into bright fall shades. Flocks of wild ducks
flew overhead on their journey to the south. Meadowlarks sang their morning song, robins chirped on tree tops, and all nature smiled out of doors
this bright sunny morning, as if trying to cheer my sad heart at parting
with my loving family. My father and I started in our one-seated buggy on
our two and a half days trip to La Villa. A stop for the first night's rest was
made at Los Luceros, where my father's uncles, Don Nemecio and Lucas
Lucero, lived in the big double house built by their father, Don Diego.
The house stood on top of a high hill commanding a beautiful view of the
Chama and Rio del Norte valleys.

This was the region of the explorer Oñate. Here with his courageous
colonizers and pious friars, Oñate founded the first Spanish settlement and
built the first church near San Juan de Los Cabelleros, and started a culture
of religion, arts, and science in the New Spain, even before the Atlantic
seaboard was settled. The industries of weaving and wood carving started
here. His craftsmen carried in their minds their patterns depicting a true
artistic talent. The Spanish not being influenced by outside sources, pre-
served these arts better in New Mexico than in other countries. The first
Spanish drama of *"Los Moros"* was given during the dedication of the
church.

From Taos we traveled over the old road, *"El Camino Militar,"* which
connected Fort Garland with Fort Marcy in Santa Fe.

(. . .)

I found this city of the Holy Faith rich in its three centuries of glamor-
ous history and still holding to many of the old Spanish customs which

injected that ancient flavor found so interesting by the newcomer. In evidence around the plaza square were the squeaky *carretas* loaded with wood and pulled by burros. Herds of these meek burden bearers went around the streets loaded with wood, *amole* root and other vintages

(. . .)

The big, attractive, old-style holes were still well-kept with their long, deep-walled, cool *salas de recibo*, and *placitas* surrounded with neat, whitewashed porches. One of these most attractive old homes was the home of Aunt Magdalena's sister, my Aunt Cleofas Garcia, on Alto Street. Another one was Don Felipe Delgado's home, on the corner of Burro Alley and San Francisco Street, where the Lensic Theater now stands. My cousin Lola took me on a visit to her uncle Don Felipe's home. He was sitting reading in the *sala* when he saw us at the door. He quickly rose and came forward to meet us. A true type of the fine Spanish gentleman he was. His fair complexion was almost as white as his hair and his long white beard. All were accentuated by the spotless black Prince Albert suit he wore. The king of Spain had conferred on his father, Don Manuel Delgado, the rank of Captain of the Provincial Spanish New Mexico Army. Only a fine gentleman like him would trouble himself in entertaining a mere fifteen-year-old girl. He showed me his family photographs and then took us across the *placita*, surrounded by spotless white porches, to the gardens. The charm of the city was enhanced by its hospitality.

(. . .)

The cardinal's visit being the first by a prince of the church to the kingdom of Saint Francis was an occasion of great ecclesiastical pomp, and brought people from all over the state.

On visits at my aunt's home I heard many interesting stories. Political topics seemed to interest her guests. The story of the tragic death of Don Francisco Chavez filled me with horror. It had happened some years before, but it remained in the minds of the people. He had been so kind to his people, and was so well liked that he had been nicknamed "*el padre de los pobres*" (the father of the poor). Don Francisco was such a strong democrat that no matter which party was in power he always won his election until betrayed by one of his party and shot to death. As he fell on the bridge he said "*Por detras soy sangre fria*" (From behind I am easy prey).

"Why don't you shoot?" asked one of the Borregos, coming up the bridge. "Don't you see that the man is dead?" answered one of the other men. Governor Thornton then appointed Cunningham to the sheriff's office and he brought several Texas Rangers to act as deputies. After a lengthy investigation four suspects were arrested and charged with the crime.

Judge Laughlin, a Democrat, excused himself from presiding in the trial, and Judge Fall, a Republican, took his place with Crist, a Democrat, as attorney for the Chavez family and Catron, a Republican, for the defense. Mr. Catron fought this case with great vigor carrying the case from court to court. The suit continued for years, ending at the Supreme Court, where the men were sentenced to the rope. This case brought great fame to Attorney Catron. Sometime before, he had, *in some way* (my emphasis), acquired ownership of the Tierra Amarilla Grant.

This grant of land had been deeded to my great grandfather, his eight sons and their heirs by the Spanish government. The deed contained a clause that no heir had a right to sell. The land was given to them to colonize or to use it as a pasture or in any other way they needed. One of the heirs sold, it is said, only his share to Mr. Catron, but turned over to him the deed for the whole grant. Mr. Catron made a great profit by selling the whole grant to an Eastern company, and the many heirs each received a small amount. The first year I came to Santa Fe, modern, two-story brick houses were very rare. The Catron mansion on Grant and the Stabb one on Place Avenue were such curiosities to us girls that we used to take walks just to see these homes with their nice green lawns and trees enclosed with wrought-iron fences instead of the high adobe walls.

*Source:* Cleofas M. Jaramillo, *Romance of a Little Village Girl* (Albuquerque, NM: University of New Mexico Press, 2000), 48–54.

## Notes

1. Especially the Comanche; see *Empire of the Summer Moon.*
2. Tomás Rivera won the first Quinto Sol award for . . .*y no se lo tragó la tierra* (see Chapter 2).
3. The Frito Bandito was a cartoon Mexican *bandido* taken from the image of soldiers in the Mexican Revolution of 1910, complete with exaggerated mustache, sombrero, *pistolas*, and ammunition belts crossing his chest. The Frito Bandito would steal your Frito corn chips to the tune of the traditional song *Cielito Lindo.* This ad campaign precipitated the creation of the National Mexican-American Anti-Defamation league and represented "a milestone for Latinos in media reform" when the ad was finally pulled (Gonzalez and Torres, 311).
4. Interestingly, the first Chicano to be awarded (posthumously) the Medal of Honor for his service in World War II was Joe P. Martinez of Taos, New Mexico, which is a large town near Las Pasturas, Antonio and

Rudy Anaya's hometown. Mexican Americans earned more medals of honor in that conflict than any other ethnic group (Morin, ref Acuña 253).

5. Murieta became the Mexican Robin Hood robbing settlers and wagon trains only after the Anglos who were jealous of their rich gold strike horse-whipped him, raped his wife, and lynched his half-brother during the California gold rush of 1849.

6. *Aztlan. An Anthology of Mexican American Literature* edited by Luis Valdez & Stan Steiner and published in 1972 included several selections from *The Broken Spears*.

## Suggested Readings

Acuña, Rodolfo. *Occupied America: A History of Chicanos*, 8th edition. Boston: Pearson, 2015.

Anaya, Rudolfo. *The Essays.* Norman, OK: University of Oklahoma Press, 2009.

Blawis, Patricia Bell. *Tijerina and the Land Grants: Mexican Americans in Struggle for Their Heritage.* New York: Knopf, 1972.

Carrigan, William D. and Clive Webb. *Forgotten Dead. Mob Violence against Mexicans in the United States, 1848–1928.* London, England: Oxford University Press, 2013.

Cather, Willa. *Death Comes for the Archbishop.* New York: Vintage Books, 1990.

Dick, Bruce and Silvio Sirias, eds. *Conversations with Rudolfo Anaya.* Jackson, MI: University of Mississippi Press, 1998.

Fernández-Armesto, Felipe. *Our America: A Hispanic History of the United States.* New York: W.W. Norton, 2014.

Fernández Olmos, Margarite. *Rudolfo A. Anaya: A Critical Companion.* Westport, CT: Greenwood Press, 1999.

Fuentes, Carlos. *The Broken Mirror: Reflections on Spain and the New World.* New York: Houghton Mifflin, 1992.

Gonzalez, Juan. *Harvest of Empire: A History of Latinos in America.* New York: Penguin Books, 2000, 2011.

Gonzalez, Juan and Joseph Torres. *News for All the People: The Epic Story of Race and the American Media.* New York: Verso, 2011.

Gordon, Linda. *The Great Arizona Orphan Abduction.* Cambridge, MA: Harvard University Press, 1999.

Griswold del Castillo, Richard. *The Treaty of Guadalupe Hidalgo. A Legacy of Conflict.* Norman, OK: University of Oklahoma Press, 1990.

Gwynne, S. C. *Empire of the Summer Moon: Quanah Parker and the Rise and Fall of the Comanches, the Most Powerful Indian Tribe in American History.* New York: Scribner, 2010.

Hollon, W. Eugene. *The Southwest: Old and New.* New York: Knopf, 1967.

Jaramillo, Cleofas M. *Romance of a Little Village Girl.* Albuquerque, NM: University of New Mexico Press, 2000.

Leon Portillo, Miguel. *Broken Spears: The Aztec Account of the Conquest of Mexico.* Boston: Beacon Press, 1992.

Mann, Charles C. *New Revelations of the Americas before Columbus.* New York: Knopf, 2005.

Nostrand, Richard L. *The Hispano Homeland.* Norman, OK: University of Oklahoma Press, 1992.

Prescott, William H. *History of the Conquest of Mexico, with a Preliminary View of Ancient Mexican Civilization, and the Life of the Conqueror, Hernando Cortes* (online reproduction, Electronic Text Center, University of Virginia Library). New York: Harper and Brothers, 1843. OCLC 2458166.

Rosales, F. Arturo. *Testimonio: A Documentary History of the Mexican American Struggle for Civil Rights.* Houston, TX: Arte Público Press, 2000.

Stavans, Ilan, ed. *The Norton Anthology of Latino Literature.* New York: W. W. Norton, 2011, 788–789.

Vasconcelos, José. *The Cosmic Race.* Baltimore, MD: John Hopkins University Press, 1997.

Villanueva, Tino. *Chicanos: Antología histórica y literaria.* México: Fondo de Cultura Económica, 1980.

**2**

# ...*Y No Se Lo Tragó La Tierra/*
# *This Migrant Earth*
# **(1970)**

*At the conclusion of . . . y no se lo tragó la tierra, the nameless narrator talks
about his desire to see all the people he has ever known and, with "great
big arms, I could embrace them all." In the thirty years since the publication of this novel, Tomas has continued to accomplish what he wanted to
do. He has given inspiration and energy to a generation of Chicano and
Chicana writers who have read him and learned from him. He has meant
everything to the Chicano world that has evolved since the 1970s, and so
much that is good in that world is a fulfillment of the visions and dreams
that move through his beautiful stories and poems.*

—Rolando Hinojosa-Smith, "On the 30th Anniversary of Tomás
Rivera's . . .*y no se lo tragó la tierra*" in *World Literature
Today.* Winter 2001, Vol. 75 Issue 1, 82.

*It must be strange to grow up in this country and not know what a grape
looks like.*

—Arlo Guthrie, "Pete Seeger and Arlo Guthrie.
Together in Concert" album, 1975.

*. . .y no se lo tragó la tierra*/*This Migrant Earth*

# SYNOPSIS

*. . .y no se lo tragó la tierra*/*This Migrant Earth* progresses like a series of YouTube videos, seemingly random scenes featuring random people. The common thread is the migrant workers' experience. The laborers in the fields are subject to the abuse, deprivation, and heartbreak inherent in that occupation while struggling to maintain their humanity. The first chapter, "The Paling Time and the Fading Year," begins with the young narrator on the verge of adolescence, beginning his period of reflection from under the porch, hiding while he ponders the "fading year." What follows are 12 chapters corresponding to the 12 months of the year comprised of a series of interrelated stories. The characters are mostly unnamed and the novel unfolds in a stream of consciousness style reminiscent of Mexican author Juan Rulfo's classic *Pedro Páramo*. It is as if the boy, also never named, is watching a flashback movie of "The Fading Year" with the reader in tow.

What that reader experiences is a powerful visceral immersion into the migrant workers' experience. In the chapter titled "Water, Water Every-where," the heat and the raging thirst of stoop labor in the strange humid heat of West Texas in April is intense and punishing. A child's desperation for a drink of water leads him to try to sneak a drink from the stock tank; the reader/voyeur feels a helpless anguish when the planter shoots to scare the child away but kills him instead.

Another scene features the happy and loving García family whose children are left alone—unsupervised goes without saying—in the chicken coop lodgings while their parents toil in the fields. Hoping to repeat the family fun of the previous Sunday night playing at boxing, they put on the gloves and the rubbing alcohol just like their papá put on them to play. Raulito, the eldest, accidentally starts a fire while cooking their breakfast, the alcohol spreads the flames quickly. Only he survives, and the boxing gloves.

In a later chapter, housebound Doña María is determined to make her way downtown where she has never before ventured alone to the Five and Dime to, in spite of her fear, purchase Christmas gifts for her children. She makes it to the Five and Dime only to become flustered and to panic at the unfamiliar press of people and surroundings. Her desperation as she rushes out the door, forgetting she hasn't paid, her shame at being treated like a thief, hearing the resounding "these damn people, always stealing something, stealing" are palpable (1095).

Even more painful is the chapter that follows the boy on his long walk home after being expelled from school for fighting. He recalls that his parents think of him as having special promise; he has bragged to his *padrino* about his ambition to become a telephone operator. And here he is! His dreams deferred against the humiliation of having to strip for the nurse's health and lice check; the racism and bullying by the other students; his shame, anger, and embarrassment at being set apart "like a monkey in the zoo" (1120) kept him tongue-tied and unable to read when his turn came although "[He] could hear [him]self all right, but the words, the words weren't coming out at all" (1120).

The principal's ruminations appear in a parenthetical aside as he discusses the case with an unidentified interlocutor, "No, I guess not, they [the parents] could care less if I expel him. . . . They need him in the fields" (1122).

The boy's interior dialogue is torturous as he re-lives the day trying to find a way out—"it's still possible; maybe I wasn't expelled just like that. I mean, what if it didn't happen? What am I going to *do*? . . . But, you know, it just could be. An outside chance. NO! What am I saying? I was there. A fact's a fact, and the fact is I was booted out. But the hurt!" (1123).

His grand dreams have been reduced to accompanying Doña Cuquita, the rag picker, to the dump.

Other hurts that appear in the novel are those of discrimination as, for example, the boy tries to get a simple haircut but gets shunted from barber to barber until he gets the message and leaves the barbershop unshorn or when he can't go to a friend's house to play because some old ladies told the friend's mother that Mexicans steal (1129).

The depiction of physical pain in *This Migrant Earth* is unsparing as families struggle with the ravages of agricultural labor. A touching vignette presents a man hoping to find a soft bed for his wife—an unlikely alternative to the usual arrangement on the chicken coop's cold cement floors. The narrator's father and little brother have horrible cramping and pain all over their bodies, they suffer uncontrollable shaking—the consequences of hard labor in the heat with insufficient hydration. There is no recourse to medical help; all mother can do is pray and light candles signifying to the narrator that "God doesn't care" when the suffering does not cease.

The migrants depend on trucks to transport them to the far away fields. One particularly lyrical chapter features a veritable babel of the voices of passengers stranded on the side of the road while the driver makes repairs, his own inner voice strident with resentment as he plans to abandon his passengers. Meanwhile, some of the passengers are oblivious, making hopeful plans for the money they will earn in the field while others curse at their woeful lot in life. Later in the book, a vignette features a conversation that further illustrates the workers' vulnerability when packed into the trucks: a drunk driver has crashed into one of the trucks full of workers and killed 16 people.

The people's humanity, their nobility, and their dedication to hard work shines throughout the novel; their long-suffering attitude and hope in life are depicted at weddings, and in portrayals of devoted parents and spouses, children's aspirations, and soldiers away at war. Rivera laces the novel with subtle and sometimes slapstick humor: a woman supposes when she hears they're going to Utah that she hears "tell it's by Japan" (1098). The workers persist and endure, working, studying, and striving for a better life.

The final chapter, "The Burden of the World," contains voices that present different perspectives from all of the preceding ones, echoing the flow of rumor and gossip. Kernels of truth rise to the surface and outcomes become clear: the man who shot the child got off "scot free"; the husband with the shakes can no longer work and all the grower cares about is his crop; Doña María cries every time she talks about her trip downtown; there'll be *cabrito en mole* at a wedding. When the boy finally comes out from under the porch after his illuminating trip through the "fading year," he is ready to embrace the world, with the confidence that he can make connections; that he can communicate and create community: "I wish I could see all those good people at once, together, at the same time. And then, if my arms were long enough, I'd reach out to embrace them all. Give 'em a warm hug" (1131).

## HISTORICAL BACKGROUND: *THIS MIGRANT EARTH*, THE MOVEMENT AND *LA CAUSA*

Tomás Rivera was working on his novel during the 1960s as he was teaching and studying, constantly striving to put himself in a position where he could help his community. He set the novel in the preceding decades, weaving in his own experiences, and those of his friends and family members. Some novels had already been published about the Chicano experience—*Pocho* by José Antonio Villarreal and *Chicano* by Richard Vasquez—but none had succeeded in channeling the Chicano experience in such a lyrical and literary creation.

Rivera was an associate professor of Spanish at Sam Houston University when his novel was selected to be the first recipient of the Quinto Sol Prize in 1971. The publishers behind Quinto Sol—Octavio Romano, Nick

Vaca, and Andres Ybarra (Romano was a professor and the other two were students at the University of California at Berkeley)—were intent on identifying literary works that expressed the unique Chicano voice and that would give the nascent Chicano movement an effective avenue of literary expression; works that would become integral to the Chicano movement, literary expressions of an ideal Chicano nation, the nation of Aztlán. As the first recipient of the Quinto Sol prize, *This Migrant Earth* represented the maximum expression of Chicano culture at that moment. Rivera worked with Romano, Vaca, and Ybarra, and modified the novel by reorganizing the chapters. A section about a pachuco named Pete Fonseca was taken out because of the character's negative behavior (he leaves a woman in the lurch, absconding with all her money). That section was later included in other anthologies as a short story, "On the Road to Texas: Pete Fonseca."

The novel was published in a bilingual format but the name of the original translator has not been established. Rivera wrote the novel in the Spanish of Crystal City, a unique "dialect, the one teachers and administrators attempted to persistently eradicate through physical punishment and psychological torture every time we were caught speaking it" (Rodríguez in Littin et al., 81). Rivera had never been satisfied with the translations and asked his *buen amigo* Rolando Hinojosa to undertake the task. Hinojosa had won the Quinto Sol prize in 1973 for his work *Estampas del valle y otras obras/The Valley* but was reluctant to do this at first. He taught the novel in his courses, studied it, and finally translated it as *This Migrant Earth* in 1987.[1]

It became the heart of the modern Chicano literary movement. The year the novel was selected was a high point for the movement: the Chicano Moratorium attracted thousands to Los Angeles to march against the Vietnam War in August of that year; La Raza Unida Party (LRUP) had a victorious campaign in Texas and LRUP was spreading to more states; in Rivera's hometown of Crystal City, Chicanos won control of the city government by popular vote with the LRUP.

In 2015, President Obama appointed Juan Felipe Herrera to be the first Chicano poet laureate of the United States. Herrera worked in the fields as a young man—like many Chicano writers including Tomás Rivera, Ernesto Galarza, Victor Villaseñor, and Francisco Jiménez. That farmworker experience was a touchstone for the rebirth of Chicano culture. The Chicanos who led the fight in the fields and created *La Causa* also provided the Chicano movement with inspiration, leadership, and broad support as *La Causa* galvanized people across the country and around the world. It brought together diverse elements of the Chicano community and beyond—transcending social class, origin, and gender divisions—to advocate for human rights, fair wages, humane working conditions, and an end to abuse and injustice for farmworkers.

When Rivera's novel was awarded the Quinto Sol prize in 1971, it was also a highpoint for the United Farm Workers (UFW). Their long struggle had been crowned with success as contracts were signed with most of the grape growers in California.[2] That the inaugural Quinto Sol prize was awarded to this novel acknowledged the central place the farmworker experience and struggle had in Chicano culture and its evolving sense of self. So much was happening, so many strands—farmworkers, students, women, artists, and writers *y más gente*—coming together to create a *movimiento* that would bring lasting change.

## ABOUT TOMÁS RIVERA

In his short life, Tomás Rivera experienced the extremes of human existence and like the protagonist in his novel . . . *y no se lo tragó la tierra/ This Migrant Earth*, he wanted to embrace the world. His childhood and youth were spent in hard physical labor in migrant farm labor camps and he dedicated himself to the hard intellectual labor it took to rise to the top of his professions, the literary and the academic, battling discrimination along the way.

Rivera was born in Crystal City, Texas. His parents were Mexican immigrants who worked in the fields in that "Winter Garden" part of Texas and then followed the crops through the seasons and throughout the Midwest. They provided Tomás with a rock solid foundation, instilling in him the values of hard work, education, and community in spite of their itinerant way of life. Early on, they enrolled Tomás in a type of cooperative community school where parents contributed financially to the operations of the school. It is at this school that Tomás learned his first lessons in Spanish, including poetry recital. He recited *El minero* possibly in honor of his grandfather who had been a miner and active in the miners' union in the Mexican state of Coahuila.

Tomás learned English at the public school like so many Chicanos of that era but did not become truly bilingual until the fifth grade, a moment he recalled clearly. Throughout his childhood up until he enrolled in junior college, Tomás worked alongside his family in the fields. His final professional curriculum vitae updated in 1984 states "Up to the time I started my teaching career, I was part of the migrant labor stream that went from Texas to various parts of the Midwest. I lived and worked in Iowa, Minnesota, Wisconsin, Michigan, and North Dakota" (Lattin et al., 54).

His parents' support and encouragement shaped Tomás into a smart kid who loved to read. His family and the other migrant workers would save for Tomás any reading material they might encounter. He recalled one particularly productive trip to the town dump where they found a complete set of Britannica encyclopedias. Another time, he came across an edition of Sir Henry M. Stanley's book *Through Darkest Africa*. He was fascinated by that account of exotic travels and found it more compelling than the Tarzan movies popular at the time (1940s). He used his artistic ability to draw maps from Stanley's descriptions in the book for his younger brother. He recalled seeing the movie version of *The Grapes of Wrath* and being inspired to read all of John Steinbeck's works. Books and the worlds they contained within their pages were Tomás's passion.

Tomás was fortunate to find support in other sectors of other communities as well. One of the renowned Chicana author Pat Mora's best-known and well-loved books is *Tomás and the Library Lady*. It tells the story of the librarian who befriended Rivera as a child and nurtured his love of books every summer the family's work took them to Iowa. She introduced him to the public library and gave him access to the broad selection available there. Despite the prejudice of the times, this woman reached out to a fellow book-lover, opening even wider the door to his future.

As an avid reader, Tomás felt the compulsion to write and leave a record of the events he witnessed, such as the car accident he saw as an 11-year-old that inspired his first stab at creative writing. Less exciting but just as dramatic was what Tomás experienced every day in the fields. He witnessed and experienced *en carne propia* "the deaths of relatives, the waste of latent talents . . . [and] the lack of educational opportunities" (Lattin et al., 64); the grievances and abuse that gave rise to the farmworkers' movement, such as working in the hot sun without access to water (not even the water in the stock tank); living conditions not fit for animals (tents, *jacales*/chicken coops); racism; discrimination and bullying at schools, barber shops, and movie theaters, were painfully familiar and became fodder for his creative endeavors. They formed the heart of his literary work and his artistry gave it the soul that touched readers, especially those in the Chicano community.

Besides his dedication to hard work, Rivera was able to rise above humble beginnings and adversity, thanks to his dogged persistence. When he was told there were no English teaching jobs available in the school district, he understood the true message to be there were no English teaching jobs for *Chicanos* in spite of his BA in English from Southwestern Texas State University (SWTU). He went back to SWTU and got a master's degree in educational administration and followed that with a master's degree in Spanish literature and a doctorate in romance languages, both from the University of Oklahoma. Then, of course, people would tell him that it must be easy for a Mexican to teach Spanish. *¡Híjole!* He could not win!

But he did! And accomplished a lifetime of firsts. He was the first Chicano teacher his brother and friends had ever laid eyes on at the high school in Crystal City. They were accustomed to seeing Chicanos only as support personnel (and not in the front office—in the cafeteria, on the grounds, or on the cleaning crew). He was the first Chicano (and youngest person) to be selected as chancellor of a University of California campus when he took on that role at the Riverside campus in 1980 (at age 45). He was the first to win the Quinto Sol prize in 1971 with his masterpiece . . . *y no se lo tragó la tierra/This Migrant Earth*. Throughout his career, Tomás continued to push himself, to teach and to advocate for his Chicano community while never forgetting his roots. Sadly, he passed away suddenly at 49 years of age (the first of his generation of notable Chicano authors to do so), leaving a gaping wound in the culture and community.

## WHY WE READ *THIS MIGRANT EARTH*

. . . *y no se lo tragó la tierra/This Migrant Earth* is set in the 1940s/1950s and gives testimony to a situation that most Americans would find indefensible and unconscionable. Rivera's novel is not a relic from bygone days, however, but a living interlocutor in a dialogue that has not run its course or reached a satisfactory resolution as long as farmworkers continue to be victimized. Currently, immigration law and enforcement continue to criminalize people coming to the country seeking work and a dignified life free from terror and despair. Roberto Suro, who currently directs the Tomás Rivera Policy Institute, states in an article from July 2015:

> Given that most of the migrants in question have come in search of work, enforcement might logically have focused on workplaces rather than the border. But, until 1986 it was perfectly legal to employ someone who lacked proper immigration status, and in that year, Congress enacted a prohibition that was designed to be unenforceable at the employers' behest. Congress also failed to create legal channels for the low skilled immigrant workers that the U.S. economy craved in the 1990s and early 2000s. Politicians, bureaucrats, employers and consumers, we were all complicit. But instead,

the migrants were designated the protagonists of this tale as if their actions alone brought about this situation.

—Roberto Suro, "The Summer of the Latino Comeuppance": *Time*, July 5, 2015

History is repeated as farmworkers contend with many of the same abuses as in Chavez and Rivera's time, abuses that have become more violent and insidious. The heart wrenching episode from *This Migrant Earth*'s chapter "Water, Water, Everywhere" is echoed in an incident recounted in the "Days of Slavery" chapter from *Days of Destruction, Days of Revolt* (the authors cite Edward R. Murrow's documentary *Harvest of Shame* in the chapter).

[I]n 1996, a sixteen-year-old Guatemalan named Edgar stumbled into the Coalition's [the Coalition of Immokalee Workers] office splattered with blood.

"His nose was so red and his face was so swollen, he looked like a clown," Benitez says. "His shirt was saturated with blood." [Lucas Benitez is an organizer for the Coalition.]

Edgar said he had taken a drink of water in the field without permission. The crew leader savagely beat him, telling the other workers that if they disobeyed him they would also be beaten. The boy fled. (221)

—Chris Hedges and Joe Sacco. *Days of Destruction. Days of Revolt.* New York: Nation Books, 2012

*. . . y no se lo tragó la tierra*/*This Migrant Earth* gives voice powerfully and poetically to a community that endures, and that survives—mostly— and that time and again must rise, must organize, must fight for their dignity and right to full participation in a society that they have sweated blood to feed.

This has been the case at least since the time of the Great Depression when John Steinbeck brought the type of abuse suffered by the Okies to the attention of the country (and a young Tomás Rivera). That old Okie Woody Guthrie witnessed the workers' suffering when he was on the scout with the others in California and lent his artistry to the task of raising consciousness about it. Those who sing Deportee (*Plane Wreck at Los Gatos*) to this day lament with a mournful solidarity the mistreatment and lack of appreciation of the migrant farmworkers. The song acknowledges the farmworkers' persistence as they "pay all their money to wade back again." In *This Migrant Earth*, that persistence resonates in the hope found among the workers expressed in conversations about the future as they wait on the side of the road for their transport to be repaired—"They talked about what people always talk about, about what to do, about what they'd do just as soon as they got there. Someplace" (1104).

Ernesto Galarza published *Merchants of Labor: The Mexican Bracero Story* as a wake-up call about the farmworkers' situation. His chronicles of real life abuse and painful, unnecessary death due to unsanitary conditions and lack of access to medical care find their literary twin in *This Migrant Earth*. Rivera's prose brings home the suffering and deaths in the labor camps, a visceral experience for readers.

The great Chicano playwright Luis Valdez took that pain and suffering and turned it on its head in his play *Las dos caras del patroncito/ The Two Faces of the Patroncito*. This gave farmworkers the space to act, and to laugh at themselves, at their situation and at their tormentors, and that action is exuberant, joyful, and powerful. Similarly, the boy in *This Migrant Earth* turns the tables on the Devil himself:

> He then cursed the Devil's mother, yeah, that'll bring him out. Cussed her, *then* cussed *him*. Nothing. Not-a-thing, see? . . . "Okay, if there's no Devil, does that mean that there's no . . . but what am I saying? I better watch that kind-a talk. I could be punished for it" . . . "There's no Devil. Nothing. There's no Devil and no nothing to go with it. No, sir." . . . The boy looked out into the night; clear, bright. And there was the moon again. Beaming. Happy about something: skipping, sliding, and gliding right through the clouds it was. (1117–1118)

Turning the tables ultimately requires the clarion call for justice that Valdez laid out in the *Plan of Delano*. The plan declares the humanity of workers—like those depicted in the novel—and their goal, their *demand*, to be treated like human beings. This community of workers is where Rivera's nameless protagonist is headed; this will be the community he embraces after the end of the novel, and his whole world begins here.

The cultural project begun when . . . *y no se lo tragó la tierra/This Migrant Earth* was awarded the first Quinto Sol award has borne fruit and Chicano literature and culture are the richer for it. Tomás Rivera's portrayal of the farmworkers, their lives, their culture and their situation came from the same place—from the shared experience of working the land, of survival, pain, and joy—as *La Causa* and both nurtured the nascent Chicano movement.

## HISTORICAL EXPLORATIONS

Both the Chicano and the farmworkers' movements used the term *La Causa*/The Cause. Both movements were born of a desire for justice.

While the Chicano movement sought to represent the interests of all Chicanos and the farmworkers focused on the extreme needs of that oppressed segment, their goals, strategies and leaders often intersected, coincided, and clashed. One place where they came together in a verdant synchronicity was in Tomás Rivera's novel . . . *y no se lo tragó la tierra/This Migrant Earth.*

*This Migrant Earth* brings home the fact that the United States has always had a romanticized image of how its food makes its way to each dinner table. The benign myth of the family farm was never the full story. The reality is much darker, shameful even, as pointed out in revered journalist Edward R. Murrow's documentary "Harvest of Shame" broadcast in 1960 the day after Thanksgiving: "We used to own our slaves, now we only rent them," a farmer declares in the opening sequence. The documentary shows how the people who labor in the fields have been the hardest working, lowest paid, most abused and defenseless workers, since the abolition of slavery. By the time it was broadcast, the hard times of the Dust Bowl and the Depression of the 1930s were a distant memory for the mainstream culture. In John Steinbeck's Depression-era novel *The Grapes of Wrath*, the Joad family loses its farm to the bank, and leaves Oklahoma for California, where they have been lured by the promise of abundant and easy work in glossy brochures.

In this way, the growers were assured a huge pool of labor, which depressed wages downward as so many people competed for a finite number of seasonal jobs. The fictional Joad family, like farmworkers in real life, struggle with abuses such as: the company store where workers are obligated to purchase their necessities (food, clothing, "housing," etc.) from their employer at inflated prices; squalid living conditions (shacks, tents, chicken coops with no running water or sanitation); no access to medical care; exposure to harmful chemicals and pesticides; and bullying and mistreatment, both physical and verbal.

Rivera depicts the heavy toll the living conditions and lack of medical care take on one family in the chapter, "This Migrant Earth." The boy's aunt has died from tuberculosis and the uncle is dying; the rest of the family has taken on the care of their children when the boy's Pa takes sick:

> So the anger that had not gone away renewed itself, and the hatred came with it. *This* time, this time it was Pa—*his* Pa. . . . He was in pain, bent over he was. Like he had the cramps all over his body. . . . You see his eyes, sonny? Watery and glassy they look. . . . he'd hear his dad—his Pa—moaning and groaning out by the chicken coops. Where they slept. His Pa couldn't stay inside the coops, though. He just couldn't. He'd choke, suffocate, he said. . . .

Along about four or so, the youngest kid got sick on 'em. And here he
was, his youngest brother, barely nine years old and drawing adult wages. . . .
The first thing he did was to throw up; and then he sat down, for a bit he said.
But then he rolled over, flat, out. (1105–1109)

These days, workers are doomed to debt peonage (debt they can never
pay off no matter how hard they work) as they are charged exorbitant
amounts by coyotes (human traffickers) to make the trip to the fields in the
United States from impoverished regions of countries like Mexico, Guate-
mala, and Honduras.

Throughout the years, the U.S. government has been complicit in this
situation. Since its creation in 1933, the Immigration and Naturalization
Service, now Immigration and Customs Enforcement, and Border Patrol,
its enforcement arm, have effectively managed the flow across the border
to assure that the growers had plenty of workers in order to keep wages
low. During harvest time, the Border Patrol would look the other way,
allowing undocumented people in; once the picking and harvesting were
done, the erstwhile workers were labeled as criminals, summarily hunted
down and deported.

Beloved balladeer Woody Guthrie, of *This Land Is Your Land* fame,
wrote about the toll this strategy took on human lives in his song *Deportee*
after reading about a 1948 plane wreck near Los Gatos, California, and the
fatalities noted as "deportees" in the newspaper. Guthrie was from Oklahoma and experienced the Dust Bowl and the treatment of Okie and other
farmworkers by California landowners firsthand (see also his song Do Re
Mi—"California is a garden of Eden / it's a paradise to live in or see / but
believe it or not / you won't find it so hot / if you ain't got the Do Re Mi")
*Deportee* has been recorded by many artists from Dolly Parton to Rick
Treviño and Los Super Seven to Bruce Springsteen and continues to resonate with those who sympathize with immigrants and farmworkers.

The program that invited Mexican workers to harvest the crops that
feed the nation then throw them back like the rotting peaches in Woody
Guthrie's song was called the *bracero* program (*bracero* from the Spanish
word "brazo" = arm/*bracero* = someone who works with his arms). After
the United States entered World War II, the government was concerned
about the food supply. The United States entered into an agreement with
Mexico that created the Mexican Farm Labor Program/Public Law 78, better known as the *bracero* program. Once again (as had happened with the
Treaty of Guadalupe Hidalgo), the Mexican government tried to protect its
citizens by including clauses regarding fair wages and nondiscriminatory

treatment in the agreement. Employers were expected to sign paperwork to that effect, but the seemingly endless supply of laborers meant that growers had little incentive to abide by these agreements. One trick they would use would be to keep the worker's papers until the work was done to their satisfaction, effectively holding the worker hostage.

At one point in *This Migrant Earth*, workers find out about a bad wreck: "That one of the trucks, one loaded with-a bunch of people, had been in a wreck. With a car, they said. That the truck was on fire, and burning real hot. One-a them new pickups—a van, they call it—all sealed up, and only a few made it out in time" (1099).

Scholar Ernesto Galarza was asked to write a report for Congress about a similar wreck that took place in 1963, a bus crash that killed 32 *braceros*. Galarza advocated his whole life to improve the farmworkers' lot through organizing, his writing, and the law. He worked in the fields as a youth and later worked on organizing the farmworkers for the American Federation of Labor (AFL) in the 1940s with the creation of the National Farm Labor Union. He was constantly frustrated by the *bracero* situation and how it made organizing the farmworkers impossible. Like Tomás Rivera after him, Galarza was a scholar, an author, and an activist. His report to Congress exposed the abuses of the *bracero* program and after it was presented, Congress allowed Public Law 78 to lapse. His efforts at advocating and organizing laid the foundation for Cesar Chavez and the UFW's later success.

Employers were also supposed to hire native workers and hire *braceros* only if qualified native workers could not be found. This clause was rarely respected, especially when native workers began to agitate for dignified conditions and decent pay. Growers much preferred to use the more vulnerable *braceros*. Even after the *bracero* program ended, growers would send contractors into Mexico to recruit undocumented people using even children as strikebreakers, scabs, and *esquiroles*.

In the chapter from *This Migrant Earth* called "With This Ring," the boy must spend a few weeks with a couple so that he can finish the school year before catching up with his parents. The couple maintain the façade of good people but are in fact thieves and murderers who prey on undocumented workers aka "wetbacks" in those less sensitive times:

> That man he works for doesn't know what's going on, and you think he cares about the Wetback? Ha! That's why he hired him in the first place. So what if something happened to him? Who's to know? You really think that grower's gonna worry about one more wetback? About a *mojado*, a wetback? (1113)

The chapter highlights the shameful fact that undocumented people have had to fear persecution from what would be perceived as their own community and is one of the few issues about which Cesar Chavez met with criticism—his harsh attitude toward undocumented workers.

By the time the *bracero* program was on its last legs, the United Farm Workers Union's original trio—Cesar Chavez, Dolores Huerta, and Gilbert Padilla—had been trained in organizing by the great Fred Ross[3] with the Community Service Organization (CSO). Two of them—Chavez and Padilla—had worked as farmworkers throughout their youth. They had suffered abuse and discrimination as farmworkers and also experienced the farmworkers' endurance and will to survive and thrive.

One of *This Migrant Earth*'s opening chapters depicts the kind of abuse the UFW was fighting:

### Water, Water Everywhere

Texas Winter Garden area heat, remorseless and humid. . . .

It was hot, and he knew it, too. But where was he then? He'd made two trips that morning, and that was it. And it wasn't enough, not nearly enough, let me tell you that. . . .

And that was it. Came that afternoon, the field hands'd sneak off-just like the kid said-away from the crops, but near enough the tank.

But the old guy found out right off. He just didn't make out like he had, is all. He was waiting for his chance, see? A chance to grab a whole bunch together, and that way, why, he'd find a way to come up with less wages. Thing is, most of the work would-a been done by late afternoon, but he had the leverage: he could always say no one was working as hard as he'd wanted us to.

What really set him off was a kid. The little guy couldn't wait. He was thirsty, see, but that grower, he, ah, he got angry.

Angry at a kid, can you imagine that? Angry at a kid? Well, he was going to teach that boy a lesson, he was.

Hmph. What he did an what he said he planned to do were two different things, let me tell you that. Fired off a shot is what he did. To scare him off, he said. Can you beat that? A kid. . .

Shot that boy right in the head. Dead's dead, and he dropped him on the spot. Blood all over the place, the kid's shirt, pants, in the tank water.

Didn't mean to, he said. Hmph. That *didn't mean to* won't bring the boy back. I'll tell you that. (1079–1080)

Although the CSO had been successful at getting Mexican Americans to register and vote, Chavez felt that the really important organizing work was in the fields with the farmworkers. The CSO would not support the creation of a labor union, so Chavez decided to leave that organization after serving as its national director. He convinced Dolores Huerta and Gil Padilla to join him in creating the National Farm Workers Association (NFWA).

Organizing in the 1960s before the Internet and social media age meant a lot of exhaustive and exhausting legwork. The trio identified the labor camps and towns where the workers resided—86 throughout the state of California—and visited all of them. The NFWA held dances, spoke to people in their homes and churches, and recruited members at $3.50 each, collecting pledge cards along the way. People were often afraid to let them in, to hear them, but once they did and heard Cesar Chavez, they began to hope, and then they began to pledge and then they began to invite their friends, and a movement was born.

By the time Filipino workers walked away from the grape harvest on September 5, 1965, the NFWA had two small victories[4] under its belt but only $87 in its strike fund. Although the NFWA was not ready for such a major effort, Chavez felt they could not in good conscience leave their fellow Filipino workers to their fate. The NFWA polled their members on September 16, Mexican Independence Day, and the vote was overwhelmingly in favor of ¡Huelga! The strike lasted 59 months, almost five years—a pivotal, transformative struggle for the union and for the Chicano movement.

In 1966, the Agricultural Workers Organizing Committee led by Filipino organizer Larry Itliong joined the NFWA to create the UFW. The long struggle was characterized by Cesar Chavez and the UFW's ability to anticipate and nimbly react to challenges by employing a creative variety of tactics inspired by Gandhi and Martin Luther King, Jr.'s philosophy of nonviolence. Chicano historian Arturo Rosales summarizes the forces the farmworkers were up against this way:

> There was an extraordinary lack of labor laws protecting farmworkers. Nor was there a government agency with which to file claims of bad faith bargaining. All the farmworkers had in the way of rights was the First Amendment, and the freedom to boycott growers and strike and picket. In agricultural areas where the economy was based on "grower power," the courts often sought to limit, or even deny, those basic rights. Judges, for example, would routinely violate the law by slapping limits on picketing without first allowing the union to argue against such injunctions in court. The union's strategy was to expose unconstitutional injunctions by violating them, thus elevating them to higher courts and into the public view. (Rosales 137)

The hard work of winning over farmworkers was necessarily followed by the seemingly impossible work of winning against powerful growers.

Chavez knew that engaging public opinion would give the UFW an essential edge. As the strike continued into its second year without visible gains and members were losing hope and returning to the fields, Chavez borrowed a page out of Martin Luther King, Jr.'s book and put the farmworkers and their supporters on the march from Delano to the state capitol in Sacramento, 300 some miles. The march galvanized the striking workers and brought new vigor to what had begun to seem a hopeless struggle. It gave the workers a mission and direction. It attracted attention that shined much needed light on the farmworkers' dire situation.

Chavez astutely had marchers carry the Virgin of Guadalupe's standard alongside the UFW's distinctive black eagle. The UFW banner was a simple but powerful design created by Cesar's brother Richard, no artist but he made an eagle out of black rectangles. It was a striking banner with its black Aztec eagle within a white circle on a red flag. Waving alongside the Aztec eagle was the classic image of the Virgin of Guadalupe, revered by Catholics throughout Mexico and the Southwest. The march was as much a religious pilgrimage as it was a protest march and earned *La Causa* the support of the Catholic Church. It also nipped in the bud accusations that the marchers were Communists, arriving as they did on Easter Sunday. Both of these symbols—the UFW eagle flag and the Virgin of Guadalupe image—have transcended *La Causa* to become ubiquitous in Chicano art.

Rivera's novel aptly portrays faith and especially the Catholic Church's integral place within the farmworker community. One mother prays fervently for her son's safe return from the Korean War, making promises of pilgrimage to the Virgin Mary's holy sites (note that one is to the Virgin of Guadalupe's shrine):

> Jesus, Son of God, save him, don't let them take him away from me. NO: I've made a promise—yes, I have—a promise to the Virgin to visit the Shrines of Our Lady of San Juan de los Lagos in Jalisco, and to Our Lady of Guadalupe, and my boy carries a medal, yes, he made a vow to Our Lady of San Juan down in the Valley. (1087)

But when the Catholic priest attempts to inspire his flock with postcards of a cathedral, he is nonplussed when they deface the cards with graffiti artists' *con safos* signature:

> [J]ust before *la raza*—the people—headed Up North, the priest'd come over and start blessing the cars and trucks: five bucks a shot. And one time, he made out pretty good . . . good enough to go to Barcelona . . . to see his folks.

> . . .he brought back some postcards; one-a them showed this big old church. . . . People'd admire the cards, look hard at that *cath*-edral, see; and then—just maybe—then they'd get to working for one just like it, is what he thought. . . . Well, sir, wasn't long before someone . . . takes to writing on them cards . . . with crosses and everything, a line here, another there and writing *con safos*, ha! . . .
>
> The priest, he just couldn't understand it; called it a sin and a shame, a *sacrilege*. (1097–1098)

And the terrible things that happen to his family sorely test the boy's faith:

> . . . angrier when he'd hear both of them begging for God's help . . .
>
> "God's help? What? God doesn't care, Ma. He doesn't. Not about us, He doesn't. . . . And not about the poor. No."
>
> "No, no, no, sonny. You mustn't talk that way. You mustn't say that. Don't you *ever* talk that way again, not about God, not against God. His word! . . . Yes, sonny, that's how it is. Death. Death will give us peace. And rest." (1106–1107)

The great Chicano playwright Luis Valdez, author of *Zoot Suit*, was one of many that Cesar Chavez inspired and won over to *La Causa*. Luis Valdez was already a rabble rouser when he met Cesar and was invited to join the struggle. He had been to Cuba and had trained with the San Francisco Mime Troupe. He adopted *La Causa* as his own and helped give birth to a new type of theater, guerrilla theater, theater that was part and parcel of the struggle that relied on "amateurs." He talks about taking theater back to its origins with the unsophisticated workers:

> We started in a broken-down shack in Delano, California, which was the strike office for Cesar Chavez' farm workers' union. At a meeting there one night Luis Valdez, who became our director, was trying to explain theater to a group of farm workers, most of whom had never seen a play. He hung signs around people's necks, with the names of familiar character types: scab, striker, boss, etc. They started to act out everyday scenes on the picket line. These improvisations quickly became satirical. More people gathered around and started to laugh, to cheer the heroes and boo the villains; and we had our first show. . . . Theater does not live in props and scenery—it reveals itself in the excitement and the laughter of the audience. (Valdez and Steiner, *Aztlan* 360)

After two years of working with the union, taking theater to the picket lines to lift the spirits of the strikers and around the country to generate support for *La Causa*, Teatro Campesino settled in Del Rey to expand their work to the rebirth/revolution of Chicano culture.

Although the farmworker in Valdez's play *Las Dos Caras . . .* gets the better of his *patron*, the reality for most farmworkers was and is excruciatingly different. Farmworkers today continue to struggle for justice and dignity as growers find ways (including human trafficking and debt peonage) to get around the laws gained through the UFW's sweat and blood. The undeniable and lasting legacy of Cesar Chavez and the UFW was bringing the farmworkers' plight into the public arena and getting the government to acknowledge farmworkers' status as laborers with the right to organize. Beyond the achievements in the field, Cesar Chavez galvanized and groomed a generation of Chicano leaders who went on to influence public policy and culture at every level throughout the United States.

All were welcome to join and support the union struggle as long as they embraced the nonviolent philosophy. Students from the Student Nonviolent Coordinating Committee (SNCC) that had been registering black voters in Mississippi during Freedom Summer in 1964 came home to confront a different type of repression in their hometowns that was just as poisonous. Marshall Ganz was one of those who joined the effort and became one of the UFW's most passionate and loyal organizers. Students with the Congress for Racial Equality and the Brown Berets[5] became involved. Clergy from the Catholic Church and other faiths fulfilled important roles in *La Causa*. Trade unionists from the AFL-CIO to the United Auto Workers, Communists, and women, including housewives, supported the UFW in a myriad of ways from picketing, writing letters, and fund-raising to marching and abstaining from purchasing grapes and, later, lettuce.

## DOCUMENTING *THIS MIGRANT EARTH*

### Migrant Workers through the 1960s

*This Migrant Earth* depicts farmworker culture and the untenable situation that had been brewing even before the Great Depression when John Steinbeck's opus *The Grapes of Wrath* portrayed the plight of agricultural workers in California at that time. Steinbeck summarizes the history of Mexicans in California—from grand *señores* to "imported slaves," namely, farmworkers, in the first document, an excerpt from that novel. The farmworkers' itinerant and unstable way of life became dependent on the vagaries of the crops and suffered from the growers' determination to squeeze as much profit as possible from those crops.

In the 1920s, growers were faced with the threat of losing that pool of cheap labor as immigrants were targeted for exclusionary legislation. The second document lauds Mexican workers in order to justify their continued availability as needed, insisting that these workers are fairly compensated and do the work that white workers are "constitutionally unsuited to perform." The growers were successful in their efforts to continue to rely on "Mexican casual labor" and the legislation finally targeted immigrants from Asia for exclusion.

The third document outlines the ways those same workers were persecuted just a half dozen years later, denouncing the deplorable working conditions and again comparing the workers' conditions to slavery. That farmworkers were never content with their lot is made clear by the final document, which is a partial list of farm labor and cannery strikes through the Depression years—from the lettuce packers in Calexico to the cotton pickers in Kern County, constantly agitating to improve their situation.

## From *The Grapes of Wrath*, 1939

Once California belonged to Mexico and its land to Mexicans; and a horde of tattered feverish Americans poured in. And such was their hunger for land that they took the land—stole Sutter's land, Guerrero's land, took the grants and broke them up and growled and quarreled over them, those frantic hungry men; and they guarded with guns the land they had stolen. They put up houses and barns, they turned the earth and planted crops. And these things were possession and possession was ownership. . . .

Now farming became industry, and the owners followed Rome, although they did not know it. They imported slaves, although they did not call them slaves: Chinese, Japanese, Mexicans, Filipinos. They live on rice and beans, the business men said. They don't need much. They wouldn't know what to do with good wages. Why, look how they live. Why, look what they eat. And if they get funny—deport them.

And the crops changed. Fruit trees took place of grain fields, and vegetables to feed the world spread out on the bottoms: lettuce, cauliflower, artichokes, potatoes—stoop crops. A man may stand to use a scythe, a ploy, a pitchfork; but he must crawl like a bug between the rows of lettuce, he must bend his back and pull his long bag between the cotton rows, he must go on his knew like a penitent across a cauliflower patch.

*Source:* From *The Grapes of Wrath* by John Steinbeck, copyright 1939, renewed © 1967 by John Steinbeck, 231–232. Used by permission of Viking Books, an imprint of Penguin Publishing Group, a division of Penguin Random House LLC.

# From *Far from Being Undesirables*, 1928

Mexican laborers who would be chiefly affected by the projected exclusion measure are so far from being undesirables that the Southwest would experience great difficulty in getting along without them. Most of the great development work of this area has been accomplished and is maintained by Mexican labor. The great industries of the Southwest—agricultural, horticultural, viticultural, mining, stock raising, and so on—are to a very large extent dependent upon the Mexican labor which this law would bar out. This region's railways were built and their roadways are maintained by Mexicans. . . .

There are around 136,000 farmers in California. Of these, 100,000 have holdings under 100 acres; 83,000, farm tracts under forty acres. With these small farmers, their project is a one-man affair until harvesting period is reached, then they need ten, twenty or fifty hands to get their crop off and into market. Fluid, casual labor is for them a factor determining profits or ruin. Specialized agriculture has reached its greatest development in California. The more specialized our agriculture has become, the greater has grown the need for a fluid labor supply to handle the cropping.

Mexican casual labor fills the requirement of the California farm as no other labor has done in the past. The Mexican withstands the high temperatures of the Imperial and San Joaquin valleys. He is adapted to field conditions. He moves from one locality to another as the rotation of the seasonal crops progresses. He does heavy field work—particularly in the so-called "stoop crops" and "knee crops" of vegetable and cantaloupe production—which white labor refuses to do and is constitutionally unsuited to perform.

W.E. Goodspeed, superintendent of the California Orchard Company in the Salinas Valley, says: "Our peak harvest demands run from 400 to 500 employees as against a normal labor demand of from 75 to 100. We have tried out every form of transient labor except the Negro, with the result that we have found it necessary to confine our surplus as nearly as possible to Mexicans." This statement is typical of growers' experience on both large and small properties. Farm advisers, labor agencies, and ranch managers in the San Joaquin Valley, in the citrus and walnut districts south of Tehachapi, and the irrigated district of the Coachella and Imperial valleys agree that at present Mexican casual labor constitutes between 70 and 80 percent of the total of that class.

California agriculture is not wedded to Mexican labor because it is cheap labor. According to statistics of the United States Department of Agriculture, California paid the highest farm wage—ninety dollars—in the country in 1926. Where white labor is available it works with Mexican and at the same wage. According to the same statistics, the average United

States wage is fifty dollars. It has been increasingly demonstrated that in certain production areas, notably in the growing cotton acreages of the San Joaquin Valley, white casual labor refuses to work at these jobs. Of 2000 whites from Oklahoma who came to the San Joaquin cotton areas two years ago, less than 2 percent finished the season.

Source: Charles Teague, "A Statement on Mexican Immigration," *Saturday Evening Post* 107 (March 10, 1928): 86–87.

## From "Organization Efforts of Mexican Agricultural Workers," *Labor Clarion*, 1934

After nearly a month's investigation, the commission delegated by the National Labor Relations Board to investigate the almost unbelievable reports from the Imperial Valley of violence, peonage, denial of constitutional rights and persecution of workers in connection with labor difficulties, has submitted its report to Washington.

The commission reports some terrible facts of "filth, squalor, the entire absence of sanitation; of habitation unfit for human beings, lack of pure water, of general discomfort which breeds a social sullenness dangerous to the community, and with many workers unable to earn sufficient to maintain so much as a primitive or savage standard of living."

But worse than all these, in the opinion of the commission, is the suppression of what we in the United States claim as our birthright—the freedom to express our lawful opinions and legally to organize to better our lot and that of our fellowmen.

Altogether, the report reveals a terrible blot on our civilization—a blot that it must be the endeavor of every citizen, and especially every official, to eradicate at once. Let us have an end to this slavery and starvation in a land of plenty, and a restoration of those rights to which even the humble Mexican and Filipino are entitled under our constitution and laws.

Source: Federal Writers' Project, "Organization Efforts of Mexican Agricultural Workers" in *Monographs Prepared for a Documentary History of Migratory Farm Labor*, 1938, 4, Bancroft Library, Berkeley, CR-2 Carton 37, folder NF 73 cited in *Labor Clarion*, February 23, 1934, 237.

## From "Organization Efforts of Mexican Agricultural Workers," 1938

### 1930

*February 11 to February 18.* Lettuce packers and trimmers at Brawley, Holtville, Calexico, and El Centro, Imperial County. Struck for higher wages.

Association Mutual del Imperial Valle (Mexican Union) and Agricultural Workers Industrial League (including Mexican membership) involved.

*March.* Not a strike, but disorder marked attempts to unionize the Mexican and other cantaloupe pickers, undertaken by A.W.I.L., organized by the Trade Union Unity League, a Communist faction, in Imperial Valley. Total of 103 arrested including nine organizers, come of whom were sentenced under the Criminal Syndicalism Law to prison terms ranging from 3 to 42 years.

## 1931

*August.* Cannery workers' strike. Santa Clara County, called by the Cannery & Agricultural Workers Industrial Union, an outgrowth of the A.W.I.L., or, as a matter of fact, a change of name in the same organization, broadened to include cannery workers. Mexican workers included in membership of union involved.

## 1932

*May.* Pea pickers, San Mateo County. Strike promulgated by the C. & A.W.I.U., which included Mexicans in membership.

## 1933

*April.* Pea pickers, southern Alameda and Santa Clara Counties. C. & A.W.I.U. controlled strike, membership including Mexicans.

*June.* Berry pickers and craters, El Monte, San Gabriel Valley, and a Santa Monica. Ordered by Farm Workers Union, also A.W.I.U. including Mexicans in racial composition. Mexicans aided by CROM, powerful Mexican labor party, which ordered boycott of Japanese goods in Mexican stores as a result of strike, which was directed against Japanese growers.

*August.* Lettuce field workers, Salinas and Watsonville areas. Strike ordered by Filipino Labor Chamber, joined by A.W.I.U. which included Mexican workers. Filipino leaders endeavored to restrict strike to Filipinos, while A.W.I.U. fought this and insisted on including both Mexican and Japanese workers.

*August.* Beet workers in Oxnard district. Strike ordered by A.W.I.U. which included Mexicans, and by the Filipino Protective Union.

*September.* Grape pickers, Fresno, Tulare, and San Joaquin Counties. Called by C. & A.W.I.U. which included Mexicans. Marked by unusual amount of violence and numerous arrests, particularly at Lodi where strikers were driven from the district.

*October.* Cotton pickers, San Joaquin, King, Tulare, Kern, Madera, Merced, Fresno, Imperial, and Stanislaus Counties. Called by C. & A.W.I.U., 55 percent of the strikers being Mexicans. Strike lasted 22 days in battle for higher wages and abolition of labor contractor system. Three killed and scores injured in this strike, which was marked by extreme disorder. Gained increase of 15¢ per hundred pounds in rate for picking cotton.

*November.* Cantaloupe field workers. Called by Mexican Workers Union, in battle for higher wages to meet increased costs of living. Although Mexican union lacked proper direction and leadership, some slight gains in wages were secured as the result of actions carried on by the Mexican organized workers.

*June.* Orange pickers, El Cajon, San Diego County. Mexican Union of Laborers & Field Workers called strike for higher wages.

*November.* Orange pickers, Santa Ana, Orange County. Campesinos y Obreros, Mexican Workers Union.

. . .


## 1938

*August.* Field hands, Orange County. C.U.O.M. members voted to join United Cannery & Agricultural Workers (C.I.O.). Struck against proposed wage cut by Japanese growers. Outcome not clear.

*August.* Lemon pickers, San Fernando Heights, Los Angeles County. Mexicans included in U.C.A.P.A.W.A., which won small wage increase.

*September.* Pea pickers, Hollister. Mexicans involved as members of the U.C.A.P.A.W.A. Wage increase demand lost.

*September.* Cotton pickers, Kern County. Some Mexicans in U.C.A.P.A.W.A. Demand for a wage increases lost. Much violence, several riots, and numerous arrests.

Source: "Organization Efforts of Mexican Agricultural Workers," 24–28, Bancroft Library, Berkeley, CR-2 Carton 37, folder NF73, 243.

## The *Bracero* Program

In *This Migrant Earth*, the farmworkers' tenuous labor and unstable domestic conditions are unflinchingly and brutally depicted. Mexicans who came into the country to work under the *bracero* program typically signed documents like the first one, a contract signed by a *bracero* named Roman Gaxiola in 1957. This appears to be a fair and straightforward contract as mandated by the agreement signed by the United States and Mexico. Unfortunately, the second document makes clear that such contracts were rarely respected. Presented to the United Nations in 1959 by U.S. leftists, this document denounces the shameful exploitation of the *bracero* farmworkers, clearly detailing the widespread abuses of the *Bracero* agreement.

In the third document, Chicano activist, scholar, and ex-farmworker Ernesto Galarza brings his memoir *Barrio Boy* to an end with a heartfelt and inspirational testimonial about these same conditions. He relates how his early exposure to farmworker grievances gave rise to his own passion for organizing the long-suffering workers.

# From *Roman Gaxiola Standard Work Contract*, 1957

1. **Incorporation by Reference.**—This Work Contract is subject to the provisions of the Migrant Labor Agreement of 1951, as amended, and the provisions of that Agreement are specifically incorporated herein by reference. Whenever the term "Agreement" is used in the Work Contract it shall mean the Migrant Labor Agreement of 1951, as amended.

2. **Lodging.**—The Employer agrees to furnish the Mexican Worker upon the Mexican Worker's arrival at the place of employment and throughout his entire period of employment, without cost to such Mexican Worker, hygienic lodgings adequate to the climatic conditions of the area of employment and not inferior to those of the average type which are generally furnished to domestic agricultural workers in such area. Such lodgings shall include blankets when necessary, and beds or cots, and mattresses when necessary. Mexican Workers may not be assigned to any lodging quarters in such numbers as will result in overcrowding of the premises. Sanitary facilities to accommodate them shall also be furnished by the Employer. The Employer further agrees to comply with such housing standards as may be prescribed jointly by the United States and Mexico.

Where it is jointly determined under the provisions of Article 30 of the Agreement that the Employer has willfully failed to furnish adequate lodgings as required by the provisions of this Article and the Secretary of Labor terminates the Work Contract, the Employer will, except as otherwise provided in the Agreement of this Work Contract, be required to pay all his obligations under this Contract and the three-fourths guarantee provided in Article 10 of this Work Contract beginning with the day after arrival at the place of employment and ending with the termination date specified in this Work Contract.

. . .

Name of employer} IMPERIAL VALLEY FARMERS ASSOCIATION

Place or places where worker will be employed: CALIF: Imperial, San Diego (Borrego Vall Riverside (East)

Duration of this contract} Jan 21, 1957 to the} Mar 15 1957

Upon termination of this contract the worker will be returned to: EL CENTRO RECEPTION CENTER

Mexican consulate having jurisdiction over place employment: CALEXICO, CALIF:

Representative of the Secretary of Labor having jurisdiction over place of employment: SAN FRANCISCO, CALIF.

Wage rates to be paid to worker are as specified below, or the prevailing wage rate, whichever is the higher: [illegible]

The Mexican Worker may be employed in other Agricultural Employment, when specifically authorized by the Secretary of Labor or his designee, and when so employed he will be paid at the minimum rate specified or the prevailing wage, if higher.

*Source:* The Bracero History Archive. Roy Rosenzweig Center for History and New Media. Available at: http://braceroarchive.org/archive/fullsize/roman-gaxiola,-manuel-de-jesus,-standard-work-contract_56bab3a428.jpg. Retrieved October 9, 2015.

## From *Our Badge of Infamy*, 1959

Each year hundreds of thousands of Mexican agricultural workers are brought into the United States during the harvest season. The seasonal demand for this type of labor has been fairly steady, even though mechanization of agriculture has somewhat decreased this demand. However, since few United States workers would consider doing the back-breaking jobs in the fields, harvesting cotton, picking berries, gathering sugarbeet and other vegetables, the mass recruiting of workers from across the border becomes an annual occurrence.

Most of these workers come from the neighboring Mexican provinces. They are among the poorest peasants in the Western Hemisphere. Often the money they can earn in three to six months each year in the United States constitutes the bulk of their families' annual income

Their treatment in the United States during their yearly stay is even worse than that of citizens and non-citizens of Mexican origin or descent.

These workers are forced to work for a pittance, to live in makeshift shacks in the most unsanitary conditions. American agricultural workers are opposed to this annual influx of a large reserve labor force which, by its low earning standard, depresses wage levels of American farm workers in the area. Those who employ the braceros are quite satisfied. The large growers make certain that "troublemakers" are quickly picked up and unceremoniously shipped back to Mexico.

During World War II, when an emergency developed as a result of a shortage of agricultural workers, Mexican nationals were sought. Under the wartime emergency farm labor program, which was extended beyond the war's end to 1947, 219,000 Mexican nationals were imported to the United States at Government expense. In 1945 California alone had 63 percent of the total Mexican workers in the country and, during harvest-time, that figure rose to 90 percent.

During the war emergency, the United States Immigration and Naturalization Service, together with the United States Employment Service, the Farm Placement Service, and the Department of State, helped the vegetable growers to contract otherwise inadmissible aliens for temporary agricultural employment.

The report of the President's Commission states that, "Legalization of workers already here illegally has constituted the bulk of United States contracting activities since 1947." The Report continues:

. . . Our Government thus has become a contributor to the growth of illegal traffic which it has the responsibility to prevent."

The Government of Mexico has shown increasing interest in working conditions of these hundreds of thousands of its nationals and has insisted on intergovernmental agreements governing these conditions. . . .

In practice, the agreement to pay "prevailing wages" has been constantly broken. The Report of the President's Commission has this to say about the methods used to fix so-called prevailing wages:

"The 'prevailing rate' is not set or determined by a Government Agency . . . as best we could determine, the 'prevailing wage' in seasonal employment is arrived at somewhat in this manner: Farm employers meet in advance of the season and decide on the wage they intend to pay. . . . Whether the wage agreed on is sufficient to attract the labor supply needed is apparently not usually considered an important factor in making a decision. . . . This wage decided by the farm employers usually weeks in advance of the work period is accepted by the public employment services as the going wage until the season opens and employment actually gets under way. If a labor shortage is certified and the importation contracts are signed, the wage rates, thus decided in advance are applied in the contract.

"If, as usually occurs, the prevailing wage is set too low to attract the desired number of workers and has to be increased after the season opens, one would expect under the language of the foreign agreements, that the revised higher wage would be paid. Nonetheless, from the evidence available to us, it appears that Mexican workers under contract are occasionally paid less than the wages at which domestic workers are employed."

The same Report calls the prevailing wage formula "in some respects worse than meaningless. . . . Alien labor importations cannot be divorced from the practice of fixing arbitrary wages which do not attract a sufficient number of workers. The wage at which we declare a farm labor shortage to exist, is the result of a one-sided bargain made by associations of farm employers."

*Source:* "Our Badge of Infamy: A Petition to the United Nations on the Treatment of the Mexican Immigrant," April 1959, Box 5, Folder 4. American Left Ephemera Collection, 1894–2008, AIS.2007.11, Archives Service Center, University of Pittsburgh.

## From *Barrio Boy*, 1971

There was never any doubt about the contractor and his power over us. He could fire a man and his family on the spot and make them wait days for their wages. A man could be forced to quit by assigning him regularly to the thinnest pickings in the field. The worst thing one could do was to ask for fresh water on the job, regardless of the heat of the day; instead of iced water, given freely, the crews were expected to buy sodas at twice the price in town, sold by the contractor himself. He usually had a pistol - to protect the payroll, so it was said. Through the ranchers for whom he worked, we were certain that he had connections with the *Autoridades*, for they never showed up in camp to settle wage disputes or listen to our complaints or to go for a doctor when one was needed. Lord of a rag-tag labor camp of Mexicans, the contractor, a Mexican himself, knew that few men would let their anger blow, even when he stung them with curses. . .

. . .

The only way to complain or protest was to leave, but now and then a camp would stand instead of run, and for a few hours or a few days work would slow down or stop. I saw it happen in a pear orchard in Yolo when pay rates were cut without notice to the crew. The contractor said the market for pears had dropped and the rancher could not afford to pay more. The fruit stayed on the trees, while we, a committee drafted by the camp, argued with the contractor first and then with the rancher. The talks gave them time to round up other pickers. A carload of police in plain clothes drove into the camp. We were lined up for our pay, taking whatever the contractor said was on his books. That afternoon we were ordered off the ranch.

At a camp near Folsom, during hop picking, it was not wages but death that pulled the people together. Several children in the camp were sick with diarrhea; one had been taken to the hospital in town and the word came back that he had died. It was the women who guessed that the cause of the epidemic was the water. For cooking and drinking and washing it came from a ditch that went by the ranch stables upstream. . . .

. . .

. . . Mr. Lubin [an *Autoridad*] did not break the handshake until he had said to tell the people in the camp to organize. Only by organizing, he told me, will they ever have decent places to live.

*Source:* Ernesto Galarza, *Barrio Boy* (Notre Dame, IN: University of Notre Dame Press, 1971), 263–265. Reprinted with permission from the University of Notre Dame Press.

## Cesar Chavez and the United Farm Workers

As Tomás Rivera was working on *This Migrant Earth*, the farmworkers were finding their own strength through organizing with leaders like Cesar Chavez guiding them and inspiring them to use that strength to improve their lot. *El Malcriado* was a newspaper he set up that was published, at first in Spanish, for the farmworkers; it was independent of the union. The first document is an early editorial explaining that the union fought for dignity and justice and to expect sacrifices when striving for unity. The union also drew strength from the support it garnered from groups such as the SNCC that were key to broadening the impact of the grape boycott and turning it into a cause célèbre. The second document outlines instructions for SNCC members and supporters on implementing grape boycotts in their communities.

Luis Valdez brought his considerable narrative skills to the service of the UFW. His plays, including the satirical one excerpted here—*Las dos caras del patroncito/The Two Faces of the Patroncito*—and his Teatro campesino channeled the strikers' energy and helped them to think critically about their situation. Valdez went on to become the first Chicano to have a play—*Zoot Suit*—produced on Broadway. He penned the fourth document, the iconic *Plan of Delano*, which was read aloud at every stop on the march to the capital in 1965.

The next document is a stirring speech by Cesar Chavez where he employs and rejects the image of workers as slaves and animals while hammering on the same theme of injustice that Valdez laid bare in his play—the fact that the growers were able to live like kings because of their unfair treatment of the farmworkers, who were obligated to live like paupers. Finally, after a long, hard struggle that was still far from over, the UFW won a contract with Schenley Industries grape growers in 1965. The opening paragraphs of the groundbreaking contract acknowledging the union is our final document, a document that showed the farmworkers and the world that their struggles might bear fruit.

# From *NUESTRO SOLIDO MOVIMIENTO/ Our Solid Movement*, 1965

## Un Editorial

EL MOVIMIENTO DE LA ASOCIACION DE TRABAJADORES CAMPESINOS ES ORGANIZMO [*sic*] QUE TIENE SUS SOCIOS LOS CUALES SON LAS FAMILIAS. LA UNIDAD DE VIDA VIENE AL MOVIMIENTO DE LA COOPERACION DEL TRABAJADOR. LA ASOCIACION DE TRABAJADORES CAMPESINOS ES UNA EMPRESA COLECTIVA, QUE POR MEDIOS COLECTIVOS, TRATA DE PROPORCIONAR LOS MEDIOS ECONOMICOS QUE EL PUEBLO CAMPESINO EN CALIFORNIA NECESITA PARA ASEGURAR SU VIDA; SOCIAL, MORAL Y ECONOMICA PARA EL Y SU FAMILIA. PERO AL MISMO TIEMPO TRATA DE DEVOLVER AL HOMBRE ESA INDEPENDENCIA Y LIBERTAD QUE LE ASEGURAN LA CONCIEN-CIA DE SU DIGNIDAD Y DE SU SOLIDARIDAD. LA MISION DE LOS LIDERES——ES LA MISION DE AUTORIDAD——CONSISTE DE MANTENER EL MOVIMIENTO, MANTENER LA ASOCIACION DE CAMPESINOS DENTRO DE SU CAUSA PROPIA, HA [*sic*] HACER QUE SE ALCANCE Y SE CUMPLA SIEMPRE LA FINALIDAD QUE SE PERSIGUE. SI QUEREMOS QUE EL MOVIMIENTO SE DESARROLLE, QUE LA ASOCIACION SE PERFECCIONE, ES INDISPENSABLE

CONSERVAR LA UNIDAD DE DOCTRINA, LA UNIDAD DE METO-
DOS, Y LA UNIDAD DE ESTRUCTURA QUE ES LO MISMO QUE
CONSERVAR LA FINALIDAD DEL MOVIMIENTO. ESTA UNIDAD
SUPONE SACRIFICIOS, PERO ESTOS SON NECESARIO POR LA
VIDA MISMA DE TODO EL ORGANIZMO [sic], SON IRREEMPLAS-
ABLES [sic]. CUANDO SE HA DESCUBIERTO EL FIN DE UNA OBRA,
ES NECESARIO TENERLO PRESENTE NO DE LOS LABIOS PARA
FUERA, SINO SIEMPRE ACTIVO, ES NESECARIO [sic] CONVERTIR
ESA FINALIDAD EN REGLA DE VIDA, EL QUE CONOCE LOS PRIN-
CIPIOS NO ES IGUAL AL QUE LOS AMA. VIVA LA CAUSA!!!!

[Translation: Our Solid Movement. An Editorial

The Agricultural Workers Association's Movement associates are its
families. Vital unity comes to the movement from the workers' support. The
Agricultural Workers Association is a collective enterprise, that by collective means, aims to provide the economic means the California farmworker
needs to insure his sustenance; social, moral and economical sustenance
for himself and his family. But at the same time [the enterprise] aims to
give that man back the independence and freedom that assures his con-
science of its dignity and its solidarity. The leaders' mission—the mission
of authority—consists of maintaining the movement, maintaining the Agricultural Workers Association true to its own cause, to ensure that it always
remains faithful to that vision. If we want the movement to develop, if we
want the association to improve, we must maintain its unity of doctrine,
unity of method, and unity of structure in order to safeguard the movement's
mission. That unity implies sacrifices, but sacrifices are necessary for the
life of any organism, sacrifices are inevitable. When the goal of the struggle
has been laid bare, we must keep it before us not only in words, but always
in deeds, that goal must become a vital rule, the person who knows the principles is not necessarily the one who loves them. Long live the Cause!]

Source: El Malcriado. "Don Sotaco," 1965. Farmworker Movement Documentation
Project presented by the UC San Diego Library. Available at: www.libraries.ucsd.edu/
farmworkermovement/archives. Retrieved October 17, 2015.

# From SNCC THE MOVEMENT BOYCOTT SUPPLEMENT, 1965

The National Farm Workers' Association Asks You, Please Don't Buy
Schenley Liquors/Delano Grapes

Over 4,500 farm workers in Delano, California have been on strike against Delano grape growers since September 8, 1965.

These California farm workers are seeking the rights you take for granted: UNION RECOGNITION and COLLECTIVE BARGAINING. Delano grape growers refuse to recognize and respects these rights.

It is vital to us—consumers and workers—that this strike be settled soon and settled fairly.

Delano grape growers can keep on avoiding their economic and moral responsibilities only because it is profitable for them to do so.

YOU CAN MAKE THIS INJUSTICE UNPROFITABLE—YOU CAN SPEAK FOR JUSTICE!

Support the unity of Mexican-American and Filipino farm workers in the longest strike in California labor history.

## CALL BY FARM WORKERS FOR NATIONAL BOYCOTT

Since September 8, 1965, two farm worker unions, the Independent National Farm Workers Association (NFWA) and the Agricultural Workers Organizing Committee AFL-CIO (AWOC), have been striking the rich and powerful Delano, California grape growers. The workers are striking to gain a just portion of the huge wealth they create. Now that the harvest season is over, the workers need nation-wide support to impress the growers with the justice and urgency of their cause.

The strikers are asking for a nation-wide consumer boycott against Schenley products and Delano fresh grapes. Inside this MOVEMENT BOYCOTT SUPPLEMENT you will find sample instructions which can be used by persons interested in constructive action.

The principal boycott is aimed at Schenley. This huge corporation farms approximately 4,500 acres of land around Delano. Schenley is the largest producer of wine and other alcoholic products under strike.

When informing your community or organization about the boycott, there is a useful fact to remember: The Delano growers are being aided in business by immense subsidies, many of which are received illegally. Almost the entire water supply for Delano grapes comes from the federally-constructed Friant-Kern Canal. According to federal officials, the total cost to bring this water to the land is $700 an acre. The farms repay $123 per acre. The rest—$577—is pure profit.

In numerous cases—notably Schenley's—the subsidized water is received in violation of federal regulations.

**Boycott Instructions**
TO ALL GROUPS AND INDIVIDUALS CONCERNED WITH THE
GRAPE STRIKE IN DELANO, CALIFORNIA.
   SUGGESTIONS AND INSTRUCTIONS FOR A CONSUMER INFOR-
MATION BOYCOTT.

Call an emergency meeting of your group to form an ad hoc committee
to aid the farm workers' strike. Delegates from potentially interested and
sympathetic groups: civil rights, church, union . . . should also be invited.

Send a delegation to the Retail Clerks Union. Inform them of the boycott, and ask their cooperation. They might (unofficially) advise a large
chain-store not to buy Delano or Schenley products. This union could
also collect all canned foods returned by the chains and send them to the
NFWA office in Delano for families of strikers.

Send a delegation to the management of selected chains and ask them offi-
cially not to buy Delano grapes or Schenley products. You may tell the management that you intend to use a consumer informational boycott but you're
forbidden by law to use threats of coercion or a general boycott of the store.

Set up (after steps 2 & 3)—AS SOON AS POSSIBLE—AT LEAST
ONE WEEK BEFORE CHRISTMAS—an informational consumer picket
in front of selected chains.

This kind of informational picket means you hand out leaflets to all customers entering the store and ask them to respect the boycott. (The upper
half of THE MOVEMENT SUPPLEMENT first page contains the word-
ing we ask you to use.)

IN ADDITION to this kind of picket line we would also like to see some
lines with signs and placards urging customers not to buy these products.
We leave this kind of picket line for you to decide where and when and
what kind because you know how you can be most effective in your area.

6.  IT IS VERY IMPORTANT—in order to create the kind of persuasive
    tension that is needed in Delano—to make every effort to publicize
    this boycott through the newspapers, radio and TV in your area.
7.  This intensive and short-term effort to inform the consumer-public
    can be the best way to build future support for California farm
    workers who are fighting for their right of collective bargaining. IT
    IS UP TO YOU.
8.  We are forbidden by law to boycott stores merely because they
    handle Schenley products. Picket lines cannot encourage general
    boycotts by consumers of a store or by employees of stores carrying
    Schenley products.

Viva la causa!

National Farm Workers Association, Delano

Student Nonviolent Coordinating Committee in California

FOR FURTHER INFORMATION: BOYCOTT COMMITTEE, 1316 Masonic Avenue, San Francisco, California

*Source:* The Movement. The Student Nonviolent Coordinating Committee of California. December 1965, vol. 1, no. 12. Farmworker Movement Documentation Project presented by the UC San Diego Library. Available at: www.libraries.ucsd.edu/ farmworkermovement/archives. Retrieved October 17, 2015.

## From *Las dos caras del patroncito/The Two Faces of the Patroncito*, 1965

[At this point in the play, the Patron or Boss has traded places with the farmworker because he wants to "be a Mexican for a day"]

| | |
|---|---|
| PATRONCITO: | What an actor. (TO AUDIENCE) He's good, isn't he? |
| FARMWORKER: | Come 'ere boy. |
| PATRONCITO: | (HIS IDEA OF A MEXICAN) Si, señor, I theeeenk. |
| FARMWORKER: | I don't pay you to think, son. I pay you to work. Now, look here—see that car? It's mine. |
| PATRONCITO: | My Lincoln Conti- Oh, you're acting. Sure |
| FARMWORKER: | And that LBJ Ranch Style house, with the hill? That's mine too. |
| PATRONCITO: | The house too? |
| FARMWORKER: | All mine. |
| PATRONCITO: | (MORE & MORE UNEASY) What a joker. |
| FARMWORKER: | Oh, wait a minute. Respect, boy! (HE PULLS OFF PATRONCITOS FARMWORKER hat) Do you see her? Coming out of *my* house, onto *my* patio by *my* pool? The blonde in the bikini? Well, she's mine too! |
| PATRONCITO: | But that's my wife! |
| FARMWORKER: | Tough luck, son. You see this land, all these vines? They're mine. |
| PATRONCITO: | Just a damn minute here. The land, the car, the house, hill, and the cherry on top too? You're crazy! Where am I going to live? |
| FARMWORKER: | I got nice, air-conditioned cabin down in the labor camp. Free housing, free transportation- |

| | |
|---|---|
| PATRONCITO: | You're nuts! I can't live in those shacks! They got rats, cockroaches. And those trucks are unsafe. You want me to get killed? |
| FARMWORKER: | Then buy a car. |
| PATRONCITO: | With what? How much you paying me anyway. |
| FARMWORKER: | Eighty five cents an hour. |
| PATRONCITO: | I was paying you a buck twenty five! |
| FARMWORKER: | I got problems, boy! Go on welfare! |
| PATRONCITO: | Oh, no, this is too much. You've gone too far, boy. I think you better gimme back my things. (HE TAKES OFF FARMWORKER SIGN & HAT. THROWS DOWN SHEARS, AND TELLS THE AUDIENCE) You know that damn Cesar Chavez is right? You can't do this work for less than two dollars an hour. No, boy, I think we've played enough. Give me back- |
| FARMWORKER: | GIT YOUR HANDS OFF AME, SPIC! |
| PATRONCITO: | Now stop it, boy! |
| FARMWORKER: | Get away from me, greaseball! (PATRONCITO TRIES TO GRAB MASK) Charlie! Charlie! CHARLIE THE RENT-A-FUZZ COMES BOUNCING IN. PATRONCITO TRIES TO TALK TO HIM |
| PATRONCITO: | Now listen, Charlie, I- |
| CHARLIE: | (PUSHING HIM ASIDE) Out of my way, Mex! (HE GOES OVER TO FARMWORKER) Yeah, boss? |
| PATRONCITO [sic] / FARMWORKER: | This union commie bastard is giving me trouble. He's trying to steal my car, my land, my ranch and he even tried to rape my wife! |
| CHARLIE: | (TURNING AROUND, AN INFURIATED APE) You touched a white woman, boy? |
| PATRONCITO: | Charlie, you idiot, its me! Your boss! |
| CHARLIE: | Shut up! |
| PATRONCITO: | Charlie! It's me! |
| CHARLIE: | I'm gonna whup you good, boy! (HE GRABS HIM) |
| PATRONCITO: | (CHARLIE STARTS DRAGGING HIM OUT) Charlie! Stop it! Somebody help me! Help! |

Where's those damn union organizers? Where's Cesar Chavez? Help! Huelga! HUELGAAAAAA! CHARLIE DRAGS OUT THE PATRONCITO. THE FARMWORKER TAKES OFF THE PIG MÁSK AND TURNS TOWARD THE AUDIENCE

FARMWORKER: Bueno, so much for the patron. I got his house, his land, his car / only I'm not going to keep 'em. He can have them. But I'm taking the cigar. Ay los watcho. (EXIT)

FIN

*Source:* Luis Valdez, *Actos y El Teatro Campesino* (San Juan Bautista, CA: La Cucaracha Press, 1971), 17–19. Written by Luis Valdez for El Teatro Campesino. Reprinted with permission.

## From *The Plan of Delano*, 1966

PLAN for the liberation of the Farm Workers associated with the Delano Grape Strike in the State of California, seeking social justice in farm labor with those reforms that they believe necessary for their well-being as workers in the United States.

We, the undersigned, gathered in Pilgrimage to the capital of the State in Sacramento in penance for all the failings of Farm Workers as free and sovereign men, do solemnly declare before the civilized world which judges our actions, and before the nation to which we belong, the propositions we have formulated to end the injustice that oppresses us.

We are conscious of the historical significance of our Pilgrimage. It is clearly evident that our path travels through a valley well known to all Mexican farm workers. We know all of these towns of Delano, Madera, Fresno, Modesto, Stockton, and Sacramento, because along this very same road, in this very same valley, the Mexican race has sacrificed itself for the last hundred years. Our sweat and our blood have fallen on this land to make other men rich. The pilgrimage is a witness to the suffering we have seen for generations.

The penance we accept symbolizes the suffering we shall have in order to bring justice to these same towns, to this same valley. The pilgrimage we make symbolizes the long historical road we have traveled in this valley alone, and the long road we have yet to travel, with much penance, in order to bring about the revolution we need, and for which we present the propositions in the following PLAN:

1.   This is the beginning of a social movement in fact and not in pronounce-ments. We seek our basic, God-given rights as human beings. Because we have suffered—and are not afraid to suffer—in order to survive, we are ready to give up everything, even our lives, in our flight for social justice. We shall do it without violence because that is our destiny. To the ranchers, and to all those who opposes, we say, in the words of Benito Juarez, "EL RESPETO AL DERECHO AJENO ES LA PAZ."

2.   We seek the support of all political groups and protection of the government, which is also our government, in our struggle. For too many years we have been treated like the lowest of the low. Our wages and working conditions have been determined from above, because irresponsible legislators who could have helped us, have supported the rancher's argument that the plight of the Farm Worker was a "special case." They saw the obvious effects of an unjust sys-tem, starvation wages, contractors, day hauls, forced migration, sickness, illiteracy, camps and sub-human living conditions, and acted as if they were irremediable causes. The farm worker has been abandoned to his own fate—without representation, without power—subject to mercy and caprice of the rancher. We are tired of words, of betrayals, of indifference. To the politicians we say that the years are gone when the farm worker said nothing and did nothing to help himself. from [sic] this movement shall spring lead-ers who shall understand us, lead us, be faithful to us, and we shall elect them to represent us. WE SHALL BE HEARD.

3.   We seek, and have, the support of the Church in what we do. At the head of the pilgrimage we carry LA VIRGEN DE LA GUADA-LUPE because she is ours, all ours, Patroness of the Mexican peo-ple. We also carry the Sacred Cross and the Star of David because we are not sectarians, and because we ask the help and prayers of all religions. All men are brothers, sons of the same God; that is why we say to all of good will, in the words of Pope Leo XIII, "Every-one's first duty is protect the workers from the greed of speculators who use human beings as instruments to provide themselves with money. It is neither just nor human to oppress men with excessive work to the point where their minds become enfeebled and their bodies worn out." GOD SHALL NOT ABANDON US.

4.   We are suffering. We have suffered, and we are not afraid to suffer in order to win our cause. We have suffered unnumbered ills and

crimes in the name of the Law of the Land. Our men, women, and children have suffered not only the basic brutality of stoop labor, and the most obvious injustices of the system; they have also suffered the desperation of knowing that the system caters to the greed of callous men and not to our needs. Now we will suffer for the purpose of ending the poverty, the misery, and the injustice, with the hope that our children will not be exploited as we have been. They have imposed hunger on us, and now we hunger for justice. We draw our strength from the very despair in which we have been forced to live. WE SHALL ENDURE.

5. We shall unite. We have learned the meaning of UNITY. We know why [we] are just that—united. The strength of the poor is also in union. We know that the poverty of the Mexican or Filipino worker in California is the same as that of all farm workers across the country, the Negroes and poor whites, the Puerto Ricans, Japanese, and Arabians; in short, all of the races that comprise the oppressed minorities of the United States. The majority of the people on our Pilgrimage are of Mexican decent [sic], but the triumph of our race depends on a national association of all farm workers. The ranchers want to keep us divided in order to keep us weak. Many of us have signed individual "work contracts" with the ranchers or contractors, contracts in which they had all power. These contracts were farces, one more cynical joke at our impotence. That is why we must get together and bargain collectively. We must use the only strength that we have, the force of our numbers. The ranchers are few; we are many. UNITED WE SHALL STAND.

6. We shall Strike. We shall pursue the REVOLUTION we have proposed. We are sons of the Mexican Revolution, a revolution of the poor seeking, bread and justice. Our revolution will not be armed, but we want the existing social order to dissolve, we want a new social order. We are poor, we are humble, and our only choices is to Strike in those ranchers where we are not treated with the respect we deserve as working men, where our rights as free and sovereign men are not recognized. We do not want the paternalism of the rancher; we do not want the contractor; we do not want charity at the price of our dignity. We want to be equal with all the working men in the nation; we want just wage, better working conditions, a decent future for our children. To those who oppose us, be they ranchers, police, politicians, or speculators, we say that we are going to continue fighting until we die, or we win. WE SHALL OVERCOME.

Across the San Joaquin Valley, across California, across the entire Southwest of the United States, wherever there are Mexican people, wherever there are farm workers, our movement is spreading like flames across a dry plain. Our PILGRIMAGE is the MATCH that will light our cause for all farm workers to see what is happening here, so that they may do as we have done. The time has come for the liberation of the poor farm worker. History is on our side.

**MAY THE STRIKE GO ON! VIVA LA CAUSA**

*Source:* Available at http://chavez.cde.ca.gov/ModelCurriculum/teachers/Lessons/resources/documents/plan_of_delano.pdf. TM/© 2012 the Cesar Chavez Foundation www.chavezfoundation.org. Used by permission.

# From *The Union and the Strike*, ca. 1965

## WHAT IS THIS STRIKE?

This strike is all the farm workers standing up together and saying FROM THIS DAY WE DEMAND TO BE TREATED LIKE THE MEN WE ARE! We are not slaves and we are not animals. And we are not alone.

This strike is good men standing side by side and telling the growers WE WILL NO LONGER WORK FOR LOW WAGES! We are not afraid of the growers because we are strong. We want a union contract that will guarantee us our jobs.

This strike is all farm workers telling the growers WE WILL NO LONGER WORK FOR YOU UNTIL WE CAN SHARE IN THE GREAT DEAL OF MONEY YOU HAVE MADE! You live in big, warm homes and we live in boxes. You have plenty to eat while our children work in your fields. You wear good clothing while we are dressed in rags. Your wives are free to make a good home while our wives work in the fields. We do the work and you make most of the money. THIS GREAT INEQUALITY MUST END!

This strike is to force the growers to RECOGNIZE THE UNION OF FARM WORKERS! We will not work in the growers' fields until they sign a contract that shows they respect us as men and that they respect our union. This strike is a great sacrifice for all farm workers, but WE ARE MAKING THIS SACRIFICE BECAUSE WE KNOW OUR ONLY HOPE IS IN THE STRENGHT [sic] OF A UNION!

## WHAT IS THIS UNION?

This union is a group of farm workers who have joined together to win for themselves the high wages and the decent working conditions they have already earned. This union is the proof of the strength of good men who realize that the growers are strong and rich, and WE MUST BE EVEN STRONGER IF WE ARE TO MAKE THE GROWERS RESPECT US! We must be strong if we are to win decent wages and decent living conditions and a better life for our wives and children.

This is A UNION OF FARM WORKERS! More of our brothers learn of the union every day, and come and join with us. We know OUR ONLY HOPE IS IN THE STRENGHT [sic] OF THE UNION AND WE MUST TEACH OUR BROTHERS WHO DO NOT YET KNOW!

We are showing our unity in our strike. Our strike is stopping the work in the fields. Our strike is stopping ships that would carry grapes. Our strike is stopping the trucks that would carry the grapes. OUR STRIKE WILL STOP EVERY WAY THE GROWER MAKES MONEY UNTIL WE HAVE A UNION CONTRACT THAT GUARANTEES US A FAIR SHARE OF THE MONEY HE MAKES FROM OUR WORK!

We are a union and we are strong and we are striking to force the growers to respect our strength!

Cesar Chavez, Director

National Farm Workers Association

VIVA LA HUELGA

VIVA LA CAUSA

VIVA LA UNION

Cesar Chavez Foundation. Undated

# From *Getting a Contract*, 1966

## Agreement

IT IS HEREBY AGREED by and between SCHENLEY INDUSTRIES, INC., a corporation, herein called the Employer, and THE UNITED FARM WORKERS ORGANIZING COMMITTEE, AFL-CIO, an unincorporated association, herein called the Union, as follows:

## SECTION I. *RECOGNITION*

The Employer recognizes the Union as the sole and exclusive representative for the purpose of collective bargaining with respect to rates of pay, wages, hours of employment, and other conditions of employment of all employees of the Employer employed on all agricultural fields leased, owned, or rented by the Employer in Kern and Tulare Counties.

*Source:* Walter P. Reuther Library, Detroit Library, Wayne State University: UFW Administration Department, Part 1. Box 18, folder 8, Schenley Industries; agreement, 1966, 1968, 1970–1971.

## Notes

1. The Hinojosa translation is used for the citations in this chapter.
2. Unfortunately, their excitement was short-lived as the growers regrouped to plunge the UFW almost immediately back into the struggle as the growers fought tooth and nail to maintain the status quo of their power structure.
3. Fred Ross was an organizer for the Community Service Organization in California and was successful at breaking the color bar in Los Angeles by getting the first Mexican American elected to the Los Angeles City Council, Ed Roybal. He had a strong influence on the original trio—Cesar Chavez, Dolores Huerta, and Gilbert Padilla—who learned organizing from him.
4. In April of that year, the NFWA had been able to get a 120 percent pay increase for rose grafters in McFarland, California (but not a union contract), and in August, the grape workers at a farm in Delano struck successfully for a better wage.
5. The Brown Berets was a quasi-militant Chicano student group somewhat modeled on the Black Panthers. Their mission was self-defense and service and they sometimes served as bodyguards for Chavez.

## Suggested Readings

*Bracero History Archive.* www.braceroarchive.org 2015, Center for History and News Media. This archive contains images, documents, oral histories, and artifacts like pay stubs and contracts. It is a project of the Roy Rosenzweig Center for History and New Media, George Mason University, the Smithsonian National Museum of American History, Brown University, and the Institute of Oral History at the University of Texas at El Paso.

Bruce-Novoa, Juan. *Chicano Authors: Inquiry by Interview.* Austin, TX: University of Texas Press, 1980.

Galarza, Ernesto. *Barrio Boy.* Notre Dame, IN: University of Notre Dame Press, 1971. Galarza recounts his childhood up until the time he enters high school.

Galarza, Ernesto. *Merchants of Labor.* Santa Barbara, CA: McNally and Loftin, 1964. The first comprehensive examination of the *bracero* program or Public Law 78.

Gómez Quiñones, Juan. *Chicano Politics: Reality & Promise 1940–1990.* Albuquerque, NM: University of New Mexico Press, 1990. A candid analysis of 50 years of Chicano politics.

Guthrie, Woody. "Plane Wreck at Los Gatos. Deportees." © 1961 (renewed) by Woody Guthrie Publications & TRO-Ludlow Music (BMI).

Hedges, Chris and Joe Sacco. *Days of Destruction: Days of Revolt.* New York: Nation Books, 2012. This book is innovative in that it contains cartoon/graphic style illustrations of the chapters; this makes the narrative dynamic and immediate. The chapter "Days of Slavery" presents the situation of present-day farmworkers.

Hinojosa, Rolando. *The Valley/Estampas Del Valle.* Houston, TX: Arte Público Press, 2014. The prize-winning novel by the author who translated *This Migrant Earth* from the original Spanish. This novel won the third Quinto Sol prize and was also awarded the Casa de las Américas prize in Cuba. It is the brilliant depiction of a Texas-Mexico border community and kicked off Hinojosa's *Klail City Death Trip* series.

Lattin, Vernon E., Rolando Hinojosa, and Gary D. Keller, eds. *Tomás Rivera 1935–1984: The Man and His Work.* Tempe, AZ: Bilingual Press, 1988.

Murrow, Edward R. *Harvest of Shame.* CBS News. https://www.youtube.com/watch?v=yJTVF_dya7E. Accessed July 1, 2015. This documentary was the first in-depth news coverage of farmworkers presented to the general public and had a strong impact on their image.

Pawel, Miriam. *The Crusades of Cesar Chavez: A Biography.* New York: Bloomsbury Press, 2014. A frank and exhaustive biography of the Chicano leader.

*Plan de Delano*, Latinopia.com. http://latinopia.com/latino-history/plan-de-delano/. Accessed April 15, 2015.

Rivera, Tomás. *This Migrant Earth*, trans. Rolando Hinojosa. In *The Norton Anthology of Latino Literature*, edited by Ilan Stavans. New York: W.W. Norton, 2011.

Rodríguez, Alfonso, "Tomás Rivera: The Creation of the Chicano Experience in Fiction" in *Tomás Rivera 1935–1984: The Man and His Work*, edited by Vernon E. Lattin, Rolando Hinojosa, and Gary D. Keller, 81. Tempe, AZ: Bilingual Press, 1988.

Rosales, F. Arturo. *Chicano! The History of the Mexican American Civil Rights Movement.* Houston, TX: Arte Público Press, 1997.

Rosales, F. Arturo. *Testimonio. A Documentary History of the Mexican American Struggle for Civil Rights.* Houston, TX: Arte Público Press, 2000.

Steinbeck, John. *The Grapes of Wrath.* New York: Penguin Books, 2006. The classic that inspired the film of the same name and first brought public awareness of the farmworkers' plight.

Suro, Roberto. "The Summer of the Latino Comeuppance." *Time*, July 5, 2015. http://time.com/3945565/the-summer-of-the-latino-comeuppance. Accessed August 8, 2015.

Valdez, Luis and El Teatro Campesino. *Actos.* San Juan Bautista, CA: La Cucaracha Press, 1971.

Valdez, Luis and Stan Steiner, eds. *Aztlan: An Anthology of Mexican American Literature.* New York: Vintage Books, 1972.

3

# *The Revolt of the Cockroach People (1973)*

*Middle-aged housewives who had never thought of themselves as anything but lame-status "Mexican-Americans" just trying to get by in a mean Gringo world they never made suddenly found themselves shouting "Viva La Raza" in public. And their husbands—quiet Safeway clerks and lawn-care salesmen, the lowest and most expendable cadres in the Great Gabacho economic machine—were volunteering to testify; yes, to stand up in court, or wherever, and calling themselves Chicanos.*
> —Hunter S. Thompson, "Strange Rumblings in Aztlan," 1971

## SYNOPSIS

Oscar Z. Acosta's book takes place right smack in the middle of the chaos of late 1960s' Los Angeles, California. All of the tropes of those turbulent and idealistic days appear in this novel: mind-altering substances, militants, protest marches, bombings, "free" love, Vietnam, and the Kennedys. The obligatory disclaimer on the copyright page advises the reader that she or he is about to embark on a work of fiction, yet anyone familiar with the history of the 1960s will recognize historic events and many more venerated heroes and infamous villains than the "public officials" noted in the disclaimer.

The book is dedicated to three women,[1] including the iconic Chicana folk singer Joan Baez, and is followed by an acknowledgment from the author Oscar Z. Acosta, "Chicano lawyer." The frontispiece is a reproduction of the poster used for Acosta's campaign for sheriff of Los Angeles County. It is an Aztec style illustration of a buffalo under a caption that states, "La Raza Unida" and at the bottom, "O. Zeta Acosta for sheriff." The book opens with our first-person narrator placing us on "Christmas Eve in the year of Huitzilopochtli,[2] 1969" (11). So many contradictions before we, as readers, even turn one page! Is this fiction or is it history? Is O. Zeta Acosta our narrator? No, since we are shortly introduced to Buffalo Z. Brown, the lawyer "walking around giving orders like a drill sergeant" (11) and telling this story.

The first scene plays out at St. Basil's Cathedral during the Christmas Eve riot. The Chicanos are pushing to gain entrance to midnight mass at that gleaming bastion for wealthy white Catholics. They are repulsed by deputies disguised as ushers in a violent brawl that takes place under the sacred strains of Christmas hymns, Chicano *gritos* of *Viva la raza!* and demands to "Let the poor people in"! At the end of that brutal night, at 3 a.m. Christmas morning, "all [his] friends . . . bleeding in their cells, heads battered, arms hanging limp from the clubs of the pigs . . ., " (20) Brown makes a telephone call to his "bald-headed journalist" friend Stonewall to tell him the story of what took place that night. Stonewall, after cursing, mumbling, and coughing, finally asks to record him on tape and Brown agrees because he wants to get the word out about "the first religious war in America" (21).

This exchange places us firmly in "gonzo" territory, Stonewall being Acosta's fictional version of Hunter S. Thompson, the author of *Fear and Loathing in Las Vegas*, credited with inventing the gonzo style of reporting. The style is subjective, finding its truth in emotions as opposed to stodgy, traditional, ostensibly objective journalism. Gonzo journalists or writers participated in and even influenced the events they were relating. In this case, *The Revolt of the Cockroach People* becomes Acosta's gonzo account of the events that took place in Los Angeles throughout 1968–1970.

Our unreliable narrator, Buffalo Z. Brown, Chicano lawyer, shares many traits and life experiences with author Acosta: Besides both being Chicano lawyers and having the same middle initial, they share the same body type—large—and taste in clothing—flamboyant—and other qualities including ulcers, heavy drinking, and drug use. Readers familiar with

Acosta's previous book *Autobiography of a Brown Buffalo* would know that Buffalo Z. Brown resolved his struggles with identity at the end of that book by embracing his Chicano self.

This Chicano alter ego (Brown) makes his way to Los Angeles to gather material for a book and is set on his course of leadership by an early meeting with Cesar Chavez (during the final stages of his iconic hunger strike, no fictional stand-in here). In Chavez's chapel, Brown catches sight of the poem that articulates his own yearning for heroism:

> La vida no es la que vivimos,
> La vida es el honor y el recuerdo.
> Por eso más vale morir
> Con el pueblo vivo,
> Y no vivir
> Con el pueblo muerto.
> Life is not as it seems,
> Life is pride and personal history.
> Thus it is better that one die
> And that the people should live,
> Rather than one live
> And the people die.
>
> Lopitos<br>Acapulco, Gro. 1960

Buffalo Z. Brown encounters the poem again later in the book, after his failed campaign for sheriff (he came in second place!). He is visiting his brother Jesus and partying in Acapulco when Jesus challenges him about his support of the Chicano movement. Acosta's real-life brother's name was Robert or Bob, so we can take his fictional stand-in's name as significant. Jesus takes him to the monument commemorating a former mayor of Acapulco, Lopitos, a humble campesino who brought his people to a scenic mountaintop in order to take it back from a gringo millionaire. He fought a long, hard battle but was ultimately assassinated. Brown defends his own actions in the Chicano movement—he "got in some licks"—but Jesus is not convinced that the Chicanos are ready to die and give all for their cause, as Lopitos did. While Brown is in Acapulco, he reads about the Chicano Moratorium protest march and rally. He is moved on learning that the rally turned into a riot and that the movement gained its first martyr in *L.A. Times* reporter Rolando Zanzibar (fictional alter ego for venerated *L.A. Times* reporter Ruben Salazar), a person whom Brown respected for reporting the truth with courage and conviction.

Besides Cesar Chavez and Zanzibar/Salazar who interviews, supports, and warns Brown about the dangers of challenging the powers that be, Buffalo Z. Brown interacts with other progressive leaders of the time. He leads the inquiry into Zanzibar's death, defends Corky Gonzales, and works with Angela Davis; "The most famous Chicano of them all"—Anthony Quinn—supports him in his run for sheriff. But Brown's constituents are the people, the pueblo, the students, *los vatos locos*, and the militants—"the little beasts that everyone steps on" (135).

When he seeks out the Chicano militants (the fictional stand-in group for the Chicano Liberation Front) at the beginning, Brown is carried away by the energy and passion of the incipient movement. The law degree and license he got just "to prove that even a fat brown Chicano could do it" (24) enable him to take on the role of defender and leader.

The high school students are the first to take to the streets protesting the conditions and their treatment in the schools in the Walk Outs[3] with the support of the militants, the community, and the *vatos locos*. After walking out of school to march in protest, they are beaten, arrested, and outrageously charged with conspiracy, a charge that could put them in jail for up to 40 years—an example of the heavy-handed tactics the powers that be are willing to use when their grip on power is threatened.

The high emotions and bloody scenes of violence are potent and found at regular intervals throughout the book:

> "VIVA LA RAZA! . . .
>     Big burly cops with shotguns on their shoulders jump out of the cars. . . .
>     The cops begin to prod slow students with their clubs. Then there are a couple of swings. I see a kid with a blue beanie strike back. Down he goes. A long black club strikes him down like a twig. . . .
>     The cops are beginning to swing harder now. I see a girl in an orange poncho go down. A cop picks her up and she swings her purse in his face. Several boys rush to her defense but are beaten back by other cops. . .
>     Tears are in my eyes. I am breathing with difficulty. I am in the midst of the first major public action by the Chicano community. (39–41)

Brown takes the East LA 13 case (as it became known) as defending counsel for the students. Once he commits to the movement, Brown leads sit-ins, organizes protest marches, and defends the militants in court. And when he becomes disillusioned by the legal system and frustrated by the ineffectual potential for change through the courts, Brown takes direct action in the form of bombings with the help of the *vato loco* militants.

The Robert Fernandez autopsy and trial is another devastating experience that takes Brown to that dark place. Fernandez died in prison, a suicide according to the Los Angeles sheriff's office. Robert's family is convinced otherwise, that he died from a prison beating. From the exciting courtroom drama, it is evident to us that Robert's death occurred under very suspicious circumstances. But Brown proves ineffectual against the legal machinery of the state and is defeated in spite of the autopsy he naively hopes will prove his case. He is obligated to participate and even direct the proceedings under the guidance of Los Angeles's infamous "coroner to the stars," Thomas Noguchi, appearing as himself in this narrative. Fernandez's body is subjected to a grisly dissection, which (in hindsight) predictably leads the experts to determine that "the physical evidence is inconclusive" (105). Brown is deeply affected by this farce and his narration becomes hysterical: "Chomp, chomp, chomp . . . Hack, hack, chuck, chuck, chud, chomp! (103). I, Mr. Buffalo Z. Brown. Me, I ordered those white men to cut up the brown body of that Chicano boy, just another expendable Chicano" (104). The judge rules that Robert's death was a suicide—"because Robert was a poor, screwed-up Chicano, he probably committed suicide" (116). We readers do not see this as a reason to commit suicide even though Fernandez was a frequent inmate.[4]

Brown is giving a press conference about the trial's outcome the first time he meets Rolando Zanzibar: "I am too weary. I left the courtroom in a rage, bawling in front of the reporters" (119). In true gonzo fashion, Brown is always heavily invested emotionally in every proceeding—in the courtroom and on the streets; there is never any pretense at maintaining objectivity.

These courtroom battles are colorful and sometimes hilarious scenes where Brown shines as a lawyer disdainful of the system and unafraid of going to jail for contempt. A typical exchange that takes place during the St. Basil 21 trial:

"Mr. Brown, if you continue to talk after I've told you to stop, I'll hold you in contempt once again."
"May I make a motion?"
"No."
"May I present argument as to what my motion would be?"
"No. We will continue with the trial. Bring in the jury."
"Your honor, I'd like to record an objection."
"We will proceed. Mr. Brown. Now sit down."
"Why do I have to sit down?"

The judge removes his glasses. He looks down on me. His green eyes glitter. "Because I have ordered you to sit down."

"But there isn't any reason for it. The jury isn't even in here. You're trying to intimidate me, Judge."

"Mr. Brown, I don't want to hear any more of your sass. . . . Now, you sit down this minute or I'll have the bailiff remove you."

"I wish to make a motion for a mistrial, your honor."

"Not now." (143)

Brown subpoenas 100+ judges in an attempt to demonstrate the racism endemic to the grand jury process and the legal system itself. A judge brings up the subject of "Who then are these so-called Chicanos?" (219). Brown proceeds to enlighten the judges about the status of Chicanos as an oppressed people in their own occupied land; almost buried in this exchange is one of Oscar Acosta's enduring contributions to trial law for Chicanos in California: establishing their status as a class subject to discrimination:

[T]he Chicano is within his own mother country. The international border at Juarez, at Tijuana, at Nogales, at Laredo . . . these lines are but reminders to the Chicanos of what their grandparents did to them. . . . It was their own presidents, their own generals, who sold both the land and the people thereon to the United States Government for something like sixteen million dollars.

And significantly, the judge responds:

This court takes judicial notice that the body of persons know as Mexican-Americans, or white persons of Spanish surname, are a class that can be subject to discrimination in connection with their selection to the Grand Jury. . . . Let's get to it. (220)

*The Revolt of the Cockroach People* portrays the raw, earthshaking events that signified the awakening of a people. This story about a person with a great heart and the courage of his convictions lays out all the emotions of human experience. While Buffalo Z. Brown assists at the birth of the Chicano movement, he leaves Los Angeles disillusioned. His final action is to place a bomb in the men's room directly under the office of Judge Alacran (Alacran is the fictional stand-in for Judge Alarcon. Alacrán = scorpion in Spanish). Brown ends the book with an "Adios!" and a promise that he will "still play with matches." This finale's promise of future mayhem is a fitting conclusion for a book that beat to the frenetic energy of the times.

# HISTORICAL BACKGROUND: *THE REVOLT OF THE COCKROACH PEOPLE.* CHICANOS IN ACTION IN THE AGE OF AQUARIUS

Oscar Z. Acosta's Chicano gonzo opus *The Revolt of the Cockroach People* (1973) captured the spark ignited during the strange juncture that was the late 1960s in the tinderbox that was Los Angeles, California, to spread like wildfire throughout the Southwest. Before he became Dr. Gonzo on a mind-blowing, culture-smashing trip to Las Vegas, Oscar Z. Acosta descended on Los Angeles with all the idealistic and evangelical fervor of "A faded beatnik, a flower vato, an aspiring writer, a thirty-three-year-old kid full of buffalo chips" (53). *The Revolt of the Cockroach People* is the story of how this flower vato in the persona of Buffalo Z. Brown, Chicano lawyer, gets pulled into the Chicano movement in Los Angeles and takes on its struggle as his own. His life and his work embodied the raging forces playing out in those years of youth seeking freedom: from the flower children and hippies' psychedelic rebellion to the civil rights struggles for justice and equality.

As a flower vato, Oscar Z. Acosta embraced the psychedelic movement promoted by Dr. Timothy Leary, proponent of LSD's finer qualities, who invited people to "turn on, tune in, drop out." Although he turned on, Acosta did not drop out. Buffalo Z. Brown's acid trips in the novel provide him with insights into the suffering of brown people on the other side of the world.

When Oscar Z. Acosta returned to California after his ramblings around the Southwest in the late 1960s, Los Angeles was home to the majority of Mexicans living in the United States, and the east side of Los Angeles was over 80 percent Mexican (Acuña 318–319). Chicanos had virtually no political power or effective representation. The schools were deteriorating and the neighborhoods festering. The police had intensified efforts against "radicals" in that paranoid time and conducted savage beatings, shooting at brown people under the least provocation.

The Mexican American community was no stranger to mob violence and impunity at the hands of law enforcement in Los Angeles. Barely a quarter of a century earlier, servicemen declared open season on Mexicans and rampaged through the streets of East Los Angeles beating, stripping, and humiliating any Mexican or person of color unfortunate enough to cross their path while the police looked the other way. That episode came to be known as the "Zoot Suit Riots" since the sailors targeted men wearing the stylish outfits, the pretext being that they were traitorously wasting fabric during wartime.

The next decade saw the battle for Chavez Ravine take place in Los Angeles. The impoverished Mexican American community that had settled there in part due to housing discrimination was offered participation in an ambitious public housing plan. Some sold their property voluntarily, some lost it through eminent domain, and others went to jail before abandoning their home. By the time the whole community was removed in 1961, the promised paradisiacal Elysian Gardens Heights project had been rejected by the city as too progressive. Instead, it was determined that the land be dedicated for public purposes. After considerable controversy and machinations, Chavez Ravine ended up belonging to the Brooklyn Dodgers baseball team and is where they built their stadium.

By the 1960s, after decades of persecution, Chicanos flexed their political muscles, which sent shock waves that reverberated throughout the country. The community began to take a stand and implement strategies for combating injustice, discrimination, and police brutality while striving for a unified front. These strategies began with young students seeking change by walking out of their schools in protest, inspiring their parents to speak up and act up. This activism spread to other groups—from the disenchanted, alienated *vatos locos* to college students to more conservative middle-class groups. In Los Angeles, Chicanos walked out and led marches, and held sit-ins, rallies, and hunger strikes. They sought change in the legal system through court cases and in the power structure through electoral politics. Their struggle encompassed the idealism and energy of the Walk Outs, the brutal reality of repression, and the hope for but ultimately frustrated vision of national unity for Chicanos. This painful process played out in fictionalized form in *The Revolt of the Cockroach People*, while in real life, Oscar Z. Acosta played a major role.

## ABOUT OSCAR Z. ACOSTA, "THE TROUBLE WE'D ALL BEEN WAITING FOR"[5]

Not a rags-to-riches tale, Oscar Zeta Acosta's life did not follow a traditional, upwardly mobile trajectory nor did it close on a satisfying ending chapter. Acosta was an intelligent, sensitive, and natural leader subject to fears, anxieties, insecurity, and alienation. "Overworked and overindulged," as Thompson called him, he was a champion of the underdog, of the dispossessed and disenfranchised. Although he shares many traits with the narrator of his two books, he is NOT Buffalo Z. Brown but a much more complex and conflicted person. He was a devoted father, for example, not at all as sexist, racist, or homophobic as his sometimes obnoxious and grotesque narrator. His letters, short stories, and poems provide a glimpse at the sensitive artist and craftsman. Sadly, Acosta's disappearance in Mazatlán, Mexico, a little more than a year after the novels were published left the Chicano community bereft of his outsized potential for artistry and mayhem.

That potential for mayhem found him stranded in El Paso after a stint in a Mexican jail along with a scolding from the judge about not speaking proper Spanish. Oscar decided to take his brother Bob's advice to check out the Chicano movement in Los Angeles for literary inspiration and accepted a loan from him for candy bars and bus fare. By that time, he had already led a colorful life. He had served in the Air Force, been a Baptist missionary in Panama, earned his law degree by going to night school in San Francisco, married, and had a son. He had also spent some time traveling the country while working odd jobs. It was during one of these sojourns that he met Hunter S. Thompson.

Landing in Los Angeles, he embraced his Chicano identity and threw himself into the movement. He hooked up with the Chicano militants who quickly took advantage of his legal prowess as their defense attorney. Although he gained street cred with the *vatos locos* (the angriest, most dangerous disenfranchised youth), Acosta could not shed his unique status as an educated man. On the other hand, the middle-class and college student activists were uncomfortable with his relationship with those *vatos locos*. He did not fit in easily anywhere.

Acosta put together impressive legal teams that included the National Lawyers' Guild, the American Civil Liberties Union, and La Raza Law Students Association and established the Chicano Legal Defense Fund to support the trials he was litigating. He made significant contributions to trial law, successfully challenging the institutional racism of the legal system in California in the late 1960s. He demonstrated this by grilling over 100 judges on the witness stand about their lack of inclusion when selecting candidates for the grand jury. When he ran for sheriff of Los Angeles County, Acosta promised that, if he won, he would abolish the department. He came in second place having garnered the equivalent of all the Chicano votes in the county. His many successes—the East LA 13 and Biltmore 6 trials, his campaign for sheriff, and his strides toward mobilizing the Chicano community in Los Angeles—were followed by some disappointments: the Robert Fernandez trial debacle so fervently laid out in *The Revolt of the Cockroach People*, the failure to exonerate Chicano leader Corky Gonzales who spent 40 days in jail on a weapons charge, and the heartbreak of the farcical investigation into *L.A. Times* reporter Ruben Salazar's death. Oscar also had to contend with being under constant surveillance by the FBI, the Secret Service, and the Los Angeles Police Department.

Before he left for Mexico for the last time, Acosta had begun to enjoy some literary renown of his own. He was an honored participant in the first Flor y Canto Chicano literary festival organized at the University of Southern California, attended by Tomás Rivera, Rolando Hinojosa-Smith, and other Chicano literati. At that conference, he presented an emotional reading of Chapter 8 of *The Revolt of the Cockroach People*—the Robert Fernandez chapter—which is available for viewing on YouTube.

Oscar Z. Acosta's family saw him for the last time on Thanksgiving Day in 1973. The last person known to have spoken to him was his son Marco in June 1974. Some people think he died in a sailing accident aiming to return to California in too small of a boat, others that he got mixed up in a bad drug deal, and still others are convinced he was assassinated by the U.S. government. And others of us like to think he's still trippin', hanging out on a Mexican beach. As late as 2012, commenters on YouTube claimed that Oscar Z. Acosta lives in Tucson, and others that he was seen at City Lights bookstore in San Francisco.

Hunter S. Thompson gave us a taste of what we lost with Acosta's disappearance in his introduction to the 1989 edition of *The Revolt of the Cockroach People*:

> There was more mercy, madness, dignity, and generosity in that overweight, overworked and always overindulged brown cannonball of a body than most of us will meet in any human package even three times Oscar's size for the rest of our lives. . . . He was a monster, a true child of the century—faster than Bo Jackson and crazier than Neal Cassady. . . . When the Brown Buffalo disappeared, we all lost one of those high notes that we will never hear again. Oscar was one of God's own prototypes—a high-powered mutant of some kind who was never even considered for mass production. He was too weird to live and too rare to die. (7)

## WHY WE READ *THE REVOLT OF THE COCKROACH PEOPLE*

I attended a book-signing event recently in Tulsa, Oklahoma, that featured Hunter S. Thompson's son Juan who had just published his memoir. He spoke to a packed house and I was impressed by the veneration and affection still felt for this iconic writer who committed suicide in 2005. Many decades earlier, Hunter's friend Dr. Gonzo aka Oscar Z. Acosta aka Buffalo Z. Brown's disappearance mirrored that of author Ambrose Bierce, supposed to have committed suicide by being a gringo (in the case of Acosta, being a Chicano) in Mexico during the 1910 revolution.

Oscar met Hunter S. Thompson in Aspen, Colorado, at the Daisy Duck bar where he reportedly made an entrance declaring, "I'm the trouble you've been waiting for" during a summer he spent rambling around the Southwest. The two kept in touch over the years and Thompson's friendship with Oscar Z. Acosta gave him access and credibility with the Chicano community in Los Angeles. Thompson's article for *Rolling Stone* magazine about Ruben Salazar's death, "Strange Rumblings in Aztlán," had far-reaching consequences for both of them.[6] Thompson followed up his Los Angeles experience by inviting Oscar to accompany him to a lawyer's conference in Las Vegas, providing Hunter with the material for what would become his classic *Fear and Loathing in Las Vegas*. Thompson relied on his tape recorder for his reporting (this fact appears significantly in *The Revolt of the Cockroach People* when Thompson's fictional counterpart Stonewall records his conversation with Buffalo Brown) and Oscar was devastated at the way Thompson had "sucked him dry" in that piece. Thompson did not share his opinion and felt that he had behaved honorably since he did not identify Acosta in the narrative. Although Oscar did not appreciate being portrayed as a 300 lb. Samoan, he was also angry and hurt at the way Thompson marginalized his contribution to the work and the gonzo esthetic. Thompson's publisher, Straight Arrow books, offered Acosta a two-book deal to mediate the situation and his own gonzo works were published: *The Autobiography of a Brown Buffalo* and *The Revolt of the Cockroach People*.

Acosta's version of gonzo took the *testimonio* genre that was flowering in Latin America at that time and gave it the freak, psychedelic treatment to produce his body of work and provide the *materia prima* for Raoul Duke/Hunter S. Thompson/Stonewall. *Testimonio* has been described as a cross between literary fiction and historical construction. Cuban author Miguel Barnet is recognized as the first author to create a work in the *testimonio* style with his *Biography of a Runaway Slave* (1966). Barnet used the tape recorder—Hunter S. Thompson's favorite tool—to interview a 103-year-old man and former slave and then wrote the book using the content from those interviews. The final product transcended the story of just one man and synthesized the history of the Cuban nation. Mexican author Elena Poniatowska used this method for her novel *Here's to You, Jesusa!*

(1967) based on interviews with an old washerwoman about her participation in the Mexican Revolution and subsequent life, synthesizing Mexican history into the story of one person/witness. In a similar way, Acosta's *Revolt of the Cockroach People* synthesizes the Chicano movement's story into Buffalo Brown's experiences.

As in *testimonio*, the gonzo genre employed by Acosta probes the place where history and fiction meet. His works present the immediacy of exchanges between people and their clashing principles, strategies, and ideas in a visceral way missing from dusty historical tomes. Although Carlos Muñoz, Jr. (himself a participant in the Blow Outs) and other historians present the facts, final outcomes, and impact of the court battles portrayed by Acosta, these come alive in *Revolt*. As we read, we can visualize and feel the clashes almost as if we were spectators in the jury box ourselves.

*Revolt* depicts the beating, bleeding heart of the Chicano barrios. Its vivid testimony—with sound effects!—of the people's pain and frustration screams for consequences—someone has to pay! Although the flavor and rhythm of those times seem remote and even innocent or naive to modern readers, the deeply felt emotions resonate still as today's Latino communities again confront flagrant cases of police shootings, de facto segregation in decaying urban schools, and the struggle to unify.

*The Revolt of the Cockroach People* continues to serve as a potent reminder of the brutal cost of struggle. Oscar Z. Acosta's novel depicts the painful disenfranchisement of the Chicano community as well as the contradiction within the Chicano movement itself—the challenges and the potential for illuminating and uplifting solidarity that provide the hope of a conquered nation. It is past time to re-evaluate and rescue Oscar Z. Acosta's work that deserves a place in the U.S. literary canon and history books.

## HISTORICAL EXPLORATIONS

Students had begun to take an interest in civic matters through a group called the Young Citizens for Community Action. Those who had the opportunity to visit schools in the prosperous part of the district were outraged at the stark differences. Compared to the lush lawns and pristine swimming pools at the rich schools, campuses in the barrio were crumbling, their textbooks outdated and worn out, students were shamed for speaking Spanish, and disciplinary measures consisted of performing degrading janitorial duties. Students and their parents took their grievances to the school board without success.

In the fall of 1967, the students launched the first Blow Out from Gar-field, Roosevelt, and Lincoln high schools with the help and advice of teacher and homeboy Sal Castro, the Brown Berets, and Chicano groups from the colleges. During one week in March 1968, over 10,000 students walked out. When Buffalo Z. Brown witnesses the Blow Outs in *Revolt*, he emphasizes the students' youth: "Young kids who chatter and twist, sucking on straws and licking ice cream cones. Young girls with their hair teased up into frizzy beehives. Young dudes in navy surplus bellbottoms" (37). This description clashes shockingly with what happens when the police show up: "The cops begin to prod slow students with their clubs. Then there are a couple of swings" (39). Finally, Brown realizes "All around me is a new breed of savages, brown-eyed devils who shout defi-antly to the heavens" (42).

Twelve students and Sal Castro were thrown in jail to face conspiracy charges and became the East LA 13. Facing prison terms of up to 40 years, their Chicano lawyer defended them in the courts and Chicanos in the streets with protest rallies and marches. Many of these students became leaders in their fields—film director Moctesuma Esparza, school board member and activist Paula Crisóstomo and Chicano Studies Professor Carlos Muñoz, Jr.

Chicano youth around the Southwest were inspired to follow their example and Walk Outs became a strategy for students and youth from Crystal City, Texas, to Phoenix, Arizona. Back in Los Angeles, anger in the community over the situation in the schools spilled over and activists were emboldened to protest Governor Reagan's keynote address at a conference on education at the Biltmore Hotel by setting off a bomb. These activists became the Biltmore 6, also defended by Chicano lawyer Oscar Z. Acosta.

Acosta admired *Los Angeles Times* op-ed writer Ruben Salazar for his fearless truth-telling. But Salazar was almost the polar opposite of Oscar Z. Acosta—an upstanding member of the community and a role model for the American Dream.

Salazar was the first Mexican reporter to work for the *El Paso Herald-Post* and, later, the only Mexican American in the newsroom at the *Los Angeles Times* where he covered the U.S. invasion of the Dominican Republic, battlefields in Vietnam, and the 1968 student massacre in Mexico City. After the newspaper brought him back to cover upheaval on the East side of Los Angeles, he surprisingly tendered his resignation and went to work as news director for the local Spanish language television station KMEX while keeping his hand in at the *Times* by writing a weekly op-ed. Salazar was one of the founding members and the first president of the Chicano

Media Council. At the founding conference, he presciently urged journalists to pay more attention to what was happening in the barrios, warning of an impending Watts-style riot.

Ruben Salazar dedicated so much of his professional energy to investigating police brutality that he gained the enmity of law enforcement in Los Angeles. He was working on an in-depth story on the topic when he was killed by a sheriff's deputy while taking a break from covering the Chicano Moratorium. Since his death, the incident has been debated and investigated for proof of intent to assassinate the inconvenient reporter. The latest consensus seems to be that Salazar was the victim of ineptitude rather than malicious intent. In the months and years following the Moratorium at least four major riots took place as Salazar had foreseen, leaving "one dead, 30 seriously injured, an estimated $325,000 in property damage (including no fewer than 78 smashed-up sheriff's cars)" (Newsweek).

This exchange between Salazar's fictional stand-in Rolando Zanzibar and Buffalo Brown foreshadows the outcome for their daring to stand up to the community's brutalizers:

"Hey, Buff, what would you do if you actually got elected?" Zanzibar asks me, after the other newsmen have left. We've gotten pretty close over the months.
"I'm just glad I don't have to seriously worry about that."
"Why not, hombre? Maybe you won't win . . . but you're going to get a lot of votes. . . . And that's power."
"What can I do about it?"
"I don't know. . . . All I know is . . . I've heard a lot of talk about you, man. You must know the police are right on your tail. They're just waiting for you to make a mistake."
"So what do you suggest?"
"Just be careful, *viejo*. Be careful," Zanzibar warns. "The establishment doesn't like to give power to people like you and me."
"I guess you'd better watch out too."
"Why me? I'm just a journalist."
I laugh at him. "Are you serious? Shit, if I'm a thorn in their side, what about you? You're doing more to diminish their power than I am. You'd better be careful."(182–183)

Given Salazar's relationship with the Los Angeles Police Department (LAPD), the circumstances surrounding his death were suspicious and brought national scrutiny to the situation in Los Angeles. This man who was "just a journalist" became a martyr figure for the Chicano movement and a community too accustomed to the police getting away with egregious cases of brutality and misconduct. National scrutiny brought Hunter S. Thompson to Los Angeles to write about the case, thanks to his friendship with Oscar. In a letter to his editor at Random House, Thompson summarizes how the case struck close to home:

> I felt it was the kind of thing I *should* get into print . . . and for all its flaws I like it. When those scurvy pigfuckers shoot me, I hope some biased geek from somewhere like Woody Creek does the same thing for me—flaws and all. The way I saw it, Ruben Salazar was a journalist, not a Chicano—and I personally believe they shot him intentionally, but I couldn't prove that (all of my research and interviews were done *before* the inquest—before the cops would talk to the press—and the only reason I resurrected the story was that the result of the inquest incredibly confirmed the story I'd put together in the first days after the murder. . .). (Thompson 396)

Both of these chroniclers died under mysterious and suspicious circumstances, both on the wrong side of the LAPD. However these two truth-tellers met their ends, their voices were silenced, and the fire was extinguished from Los Angeles's Chicano movement.

While high school students were facing repression at home, college graduates like Rosalio Muñoz were facing the real possibility of death in a faraway land. Chicano youth were being sacrificed at a much higher rate than their Anglo counterparts in Vietnam. Twenty-three percent of casualties from the Southwest were Hispanic soldiers, while only 10 percent of the general population was of Hispanic origin. (Rosales 198). Furthermore, to pay for the war effort, the federal government sacrificed social service programs. The Chicano community felt keen losses on two fronts, in their hearts and in their pocketbooks.

Inspired by heavyweight boxing champion Mohammed Ali's refusal to be inducted for the draft, Muñoz determined to make his rejection of induction a public event. He traveled throughout the Southwest to garner support from Chicano leaders. He put together a committee to implement a Chicano Moratorium on the war. Organized by the Brown Berets, the first rally took place in December 1969 with about 2,000 people marching peacefully to Obregon Park in Los Angeles. The following February, in *the pouring rain*, over 5,000 rallied in Salazar Park in Los Angeles. By this time, the National Chicano Moratorium Committee (NCMC) was born, and Chicano youth from all over the country signed on including many who had participated in the first Chicano Youth Conference in Denver. The youth were joined by a full spectrum of Chicano and Mexican American activists who rallied to protest the Vietnam War: from Los Angeles's conservative Congress of Mexican American Unity who felt that the war was an unfair burden on the community to moderate college student group MEChA (Movimiento Estudiantil Chicano De Aztlán = Aztlán Student Movement) who felt that the government was using Chicanos to wage an unjust war to the radical Brown Berets who sided with the Viet Cong (Rosales).

On August 29, 1970, the first day of the National Moratorium, thousands of supporters arrived in Los Angeles. The NCMC had prepared volunteer monitors to keep the rally orderly and peaceful. Law enforcement anticipated trouble; they were fully decked out in riot gear on every corner along the way. The rally was proceeding peacefully according to plan with only a few hiccups that the monitors promptly dealt with. When a minor shoplifting incident took place at a small grocery store, police found the excuse they were waiting for and set out to evacuate the park full of families with tear gas and billy clubs. By the end of the day, three people had been killed, including Ruben Salazar.

Buffalo Z. Brown uses the war in Vietnam as a metaphor for the riots that were born of the community's desire to protest U.S. involvement in that wasteful, unpopular conflict that was taking such a dreadful toll:

If we don't stop the destruction of our culture, we may not be around for the next century. We are the Viet Cong of America. Tooner Flats is My Lai. (200)

Whittier Boulevard is burning. Tooner Flats is going up in flames. Smoke, huge columns of black smoke looming over the buildings. Telephone wires dangling loose from the poles. Everywhere the pavement is covered with broken bottles and window glass. Mannequins from Leed's Clothing lie about like war dead. Somehow a head from a wig shop is rolling eerily down the road. Here a police van overturned, its engine smoking. There a cop car, flames shooting out the windows. Cops marching forward with gas masks down the middle of the debris. An ordinary day in Saigon, Haiphong, Quang Tri and Tooner Flats. (201)

In one of his early bad acid trips, Buffalo feels kinship with the Viet Cong as he is chased by men with rifles:

"Hey, you fucking greaser, you better get out of here before we shoot your ass full of lead."

"Fuck you!" The gods are testing me.

*Bang. Bang. Bang!*

Bloop, Bloop, Bloop.

. . .

Laughter in the back. To my heels the bastards are laughing. Big croaking laughs. Stomps in the stomach. Whiskey belly laughs. "Hot damn, but did you see that fat greaser run?" (69)

Suddenly I hear another roar. This one is a ROAR. It is a giant black bird floating above my head in the sky. It is ominous and evil and its wings wave in the wind from the weight of the bombs it carries in its belly, to rain havoc on those who simply want to swim in a dirty lake and have a little fun with some friends. It is a giant death box. . .

I left my voice and I spit at the bird, flying at the speed of sound to kill brown babies and fine women and brothers that only want to pick up a chunk of earth and sift it through their fingers.

I left a pebble in my hands. I pick up a rock. I throw them both after the bird. I run and I stumble and I pick up more and I throw them to see if I can strike the black bird before it can drop those bombs on downtown LA and East LA and downtown Mongolia or Saigon or Haiphong or Quang Tri or Tooner Flats and Lincoln Heights or where-ever Cockroaches live.

Ayyyyyyyy, Ayyyyyyyy, Ayyyyyy! (70)

From the Blow Outs to the rallies and sit-ins, solidarity and unity stand out as being important to Buffalo Z. Brown and possibly explains why Oscar Acosta felt Hunter S. Thompson's betrayal so deeply. From the first pickets and rallies he organizes, Brown talks about solidarity being essential to the movement: "Unless we band together and fight against this type of political persecution, we are all doomed" (61).

The sit-in/hunger strike after the St. Basil protests is a halcyon moment of harmony, solidarity, and just plain fun: "But we are together. And when the sun sets, we lean against each other, wrap ourselves in blankets and sing songs of love and war and peace" (84).

Brown's candidacy for sheriff is another effort to channel and inspire solidarity via the electoral process. He declares his campaign platform to Zanzibar:

I intend to seek out the support of all Cockroaches. . . . I have but one issue. I know there's no hope for actual victory at the ballot box. I have no money and no supporters other than a few ragged friends. We can hardly compete with the pros. My effort is an educational endeavor. I expect to carry my message to as many as are interested in my views. . . . If I were elected Sheriff, I would make every attempt to dissolve the office. The community has no need for professional killers. The law enforcement officers of this county, of this nation in general, are here for the protection of the few, the maintenance of the status quo. . . . The police are the violent arm of the rich and I would get rid of them. (136)

The Chicano community does rally in support of its candidates including Brown in one star-studded event: "we are in an orgy of nationalism, solid, tight, a rabid group in the dark looking at Antonio Quinn, el vato número uno . . . and the crowd melts into one consciousness and no man is alone in that madness any longer" (175).

But we are disappointed as Buffalo finds his dreams of solidarity difficult to sustain. When the Chicano leader from Colorado and author of *I Am Joaquin* comes to Los Angeles, he undergoes interrogation by Brown's crew of *vatos locos*: "Corky knows the mistrust one Chicano has for another. He understands the fear in the room toward a leader from another barrio, suspicion of a strange leader because . . . because Santa Anna sold us out to the gringos . . . because anybody who has so little is afraid to lose what he just barely has got" (211).

When Brown runs for office he does so under La Raza Unida Party (LRUP) convinced that the Chicanos need their own land and their own government. He remembers his speech during the 2nd Moratorium, the one that took place in the rain where he said: "Therefore, there is only one issue: LAND. We need to have our own flag and our own country. Nothing less will save the existence of the Chicanos" (201). This stance aligns with Corky Gonzales's nationalist ideas for LRUP.

LRUP under Corky Gonzales's lead was envisioned less as a vehicle for electoral power than as a way to raise consciousness about Chicano issues with the aim being to ultimately garner support for a Chicano nationalist agenda. Colorado LRUP held four well-attended conventions in 1970. The party fielded a candidate for governor and several other statewide offices with little electoral success.

Buff's twin brother Jesus who is living the good life in Acapulco is skeptical. He tells his brother that his participation in the Chicano movement "amounts to nothing. It's just an exercise in ego-tripping" (189). This turned out to be a spot-on prognostication of the egos that tripped up the fragile unity that had given birth to the LRUP.

Besides Oscar Z. Acosta's campaign for sheriff, the LRUP in California also fielded Raúl Ruiz, the publisher of *La Raza* newspaper, for the California assembly. He ran against a Mexican American Democrat, which led to a Republican victory in that election. Unfortunately, when they ran as LRUP candidates, Chicanos disenchanted with the Democratic Party functioned as spoilers and provoked divisions in the community.

Those Chicanos striving for effective political power struggled with finding the best way to get it, facing internal division, dueling egos, and sabotage from outside forces, that is, the parties in power threw up often insurmountable bureaucratic obstacles. LRUP succeeded in having several of its candidates elected to local offices in Crystal City, Texas, under the leadership of José Angel Gutiérrez. Texas Chicanos then found themselves debating whether to try for statewide office by fielding a candidate for governor or to opt for building electoral strength county by county. They fielded charismatic football star Ramsey Muñiz for governor in 1972 but lost to the Republican as LRUP spoilers, again provoking dissension and resentment from Democratic progressives. However, Gutiérrez built LRUP into a solid party that was able to bring about change on a local level through the power of the ballot box.

Meanwhile, Corky pressed for a national party convention, which was held in El Paso in 1972. The two competing ideologies and egos clashed from the get-go. Corky who was more well-known was confident of winning the office of party chair. Once they agreed on the difficult question of how to count the votes—individually or by region—the more numerous Texans prevailed and José Angel Gutiérrez was elected. After a brief, symbolic show of unity, LRUP died a slow and painful death, each faction going its own way—the moderates back to the Democratic Party and the radicals to the Communist Party.

LRUP galvanized Chicanos to a greater participation in the two-party system which has produced uneven results throughout the years. Two rising stars in the 21st century Democratic Party—Julian Castro, former mayor of San Antonio and secretary of Housing and Urban Development under President Obama, and Joaquin Castro, elected to the U.S. House of Representatives in 2013—are direct heirs to the LRUP legacy: their mother María "Rosie" Castro helped establish LRUP in San Antonio.

# DOCUMENTING *THE REVOLT OF*
# *THE COCKROACH PEOPLE*

## The Blow Outs

Oscar Z. Acosta's defense of the East LA 13 successfully defined Mexican Americans or Spanish-surnamed people as a class in California, a significant legal victory for the community, and during the Biltmore 6 trial, he demonstrated the racism inherent in the grand jury selection process. The first document presents one of the earliest legal victory for Mexican Americans—the court case that desegregated schools in the state, some years before *Brown v. Board of Education* did the same for black students.

Although the 1946 suit was successful, making California the first state to eliminate de jure segregation, by the late 1960s schools in the neighborhoods and barrios where most Chicano students lived were hopeless places. The situation led high school students, *Revolt*'s "brown-eyed devils" to be the first Chicanos to test their political power by taking their grievances to the streets. Their passion and outrage pulsate throughout the students' written demands for reasonable and dignified accommodations and treatment in the second document.

In the third document, Ruben Salazar's article lays out the historical significance of the Blow Outs and their implications for the Mexican American community, legally and politically.

# From *Méndez v. Westminster School District*, 1946

MÉNDEZ et al. v. WESTMINSTER SCHOOL
DIST. OF ORANGE COUNTY
Et al.
Civil Action No. 4292.
District Court, S.D. California, Central Division
Feb. 18, 1946

. . .

Class suit by Gonzalo Méndez and others against the Westminster School District of Orange County and others to enjoin the application of alleged discriminatory rules, regulations, customs, and usages.

. . .

The complaint, grounded upon the Fourteenth Amendment to the Constitution of the United States and subdivision 14 of Section 24 of the Judicial Code, Title 28, Section 41, subdivision 14, U.S.C.A., alleges a concerted policy and design of class discrimination against "persons of Mexican or Latin descent or extraction" of elementary school age by the defendant school agencies in the conduct and operation of public schools of said districts, resulting in the denial of the equal protection of the laws to such class of persons among which are the petitioning school children.

. . .

The natural operation and effect of the [School] Board's official action manifests a clear purpose to arbitrarily discriminate against the pupils of Mexican ancestry and to deny to them the equal protection of the laws.

. . .

There are other discriminatory customs, shown by the evidence, existing in the defendant school districts as to pupils of Mexican descent and extraction. . .

We conclude by holding that the allegations of the complaint (petition) have been established sufficiently to justify injunctive relief against all defendants, restraining further discriminatory practices against the pupils of Mexican descent in the public schools of defendant school districts. (194–204)

Source: *Méndez v. Westminster School District*, 64 R. Supp. 544.

# From *Blowouts!* 1968

### Student Demands

BLOWOUTS were staged by us, Chicano students, in the East Los Angeles High Schools protesting the obvious lack of action on the part of the L.A. School Board in bringing E.L.A. schools up to par with those in other areas of the city. We, young Chicanos, not only protested but at the same time offered proposals for much needed reforms. Just what did we propose?

To begin with, we want assurance that any student or teacher who took part in the BLOWOUTS-WILL NOT be reprimanded or suspended in any manner. You know the right to protest and demonstrate against injustice is guaranteed by the Constitution.

We want immediate steps taken to implement bilingual and bicultural education for Chicanos. WE WANT TO BRING OUR CARNALES HOME. Teachers, administrators, and staff should be educated; they should know our language (Spanish), and understand the history, traditions, and contributions of the Mexican culture. HOW CAN THEY EXPECT TO TEACH US IF THEY DO NOT KNOW US? We also want the school books revised to reflect the contributions of Mexicans and Mexican-Americans to the U.S. society, and to make us aware of the injustices that we, Chicanos, as a people have suffered in a "gabacho"-dominated society. Furthermore, we want any member of the school system who displays prejudice or fails to recognize, understand, and appreciate us, our culture, or our heritage removed from E.L.A. schools.

Classes should be smaller in size, say about 20 student to 1 teacher, to insure more effectiveness. We want new teachers and administrators to live in the community their first year and that parents from the community be trained as teachers' aides. We want assurances that a teacher who may disagree politically or philosophically with administrators will not be dismissed or transferred because of it. The school belongs to the community and as such should be made available for community activities under supervision of Parents' Councils.

There should be a manager in charge of janitorial work and maintenance details, and the performance of such duties should be restricted to employees hired for that purpose. IN OTHER WORDS, NO MORE STUDENTS DOING JANITORIAL WORK.

And more than this, we want RIGHTS-RIGHTS-STUDENT RIGHTS-OUR RIGHTS. We want a free speech area plus the right to have speakers of our own choice at our club meetings. Being civic-minded citizens, we want to know what the happenings are in our community, so we demand the right to have access to all types of literature and to be able to bring it on campus.

The type of dress that we wear should not be dictated to us by "gabachos," but it should be a group of Chicano parents and students who establish dress and grooming standards for Chicano students in Chicano schools.

Getting down to facilities. WE WANT THE BUILDINGS OPEN TO ALL STUDENTS AT ALL TIMES, especially the HEADS. Yeah, we want access to the heads at all times. . . . When you get right down to it, WE ONLY DEMAND WHAT OTHERS HAVE—things like lighting at all E.L.A. football fields, swimming pools. Sport events are an important part of school activity and we want FREE ADMISSION for all students. We, CHICANO STUDENTS, BLEW OUT in protest. Our proposals have been made. The big question is will the School Board take positive action. If so, WHEN?

*Source: Chicano Student Movement News*, March 15, 1968, 353–354.

# From *Mexican-American School Walkout Focused on Problem*, 1970

During the massive East Los Angeles high school walkouts in 1968, board of education member Dr. Julian Nava turned to their school superintendent Jack Crowther and said, "Jack, this is BC and AD. The schools will not be the same again."

"Yes," said Crowther, "I know."

Actually, as Nava and Crowther must have suspected, more than the schools were changing. What was happening was that a significant portion of the Mexican-American community, in supporting the walkouts and their symbolic leader, teacher Sal Castro, was asserting itself.

Few will deny that the walkouts marked a new direction for the traditionally apathetic Mexican-American community. Behind the school disorders, an unusual unity was forming which since then has solidified.

The recent decision by Dist. Atty. Evelle J. Younger to refile felony complaints in the walkout and Biltmore disturbance cases necessitates focusing some issues which could be lost in the rhetoric-filled courtroom drama sure to follow.

First, there seems to be a tendency to refer to the incidents as the "Brown Beret cases"—especially by a local wire service which called them that in its dispatches last Monday and Tuesday. Much more than the activities of a small militant group are at stake.

Brown Berets were involved in the walkouts and in the disturbances and fires at the Biltmore during a speech by Gov. Reagan April 24, 1969. But it is important to know, not from a legal but from an overall point of view that the cases stem from a genuine concern over the quality of education Mexican-Americans are receiving.

Sal Castro, who was indicted by the grand jury on felony conspiracy charges in the school walkout case, has repeatedly been defended, putting aside the indictment, which is a legal matter, by many Mexican-American organizations and such public figures as Dr. Nava, Congressman Ed Roybal and George Brown and Dr. Miguel Montes, former member of the state board of education.

Nava went so far as to tell a news conference July 31, 1969, that Castro "has been singled out for harassment and persecution" for his "telling criticism and disclosures of the ineffectiveness of Los Angeles schools."

Castro, by the way, was called a Brown Beret by a local newspaper (not *The Times*) and the controversial teacher carries a printed retraction by the paper.

In the Biltmore case, fires allegedly set by Brown Beret types beclouded the fact that many of those arrested, since exonerated of any crime, merely had wanted to tell Gov. Reagan, if somewhat impolitely, what they thought of our schools.

The very reason why the district attorney decided to refile charges against Castro and 12 others involved in the walkouts and against five persons in the Biltmore case opens important questions.

For some time now the cases have been bogged down in appellate court where the defendants contended that the grand jury indictments were illegal because persons with Spanish surnames are systematically excluded from Los Angeles County grand juries.

Dep. Dist. Atty. Richard Hecht told this column that a decision by the appellate court did not seem forthcoming and that in the interest of a speedy trial for the defendants, the district attorney's office had decided to ask that the present cases on appeal be dismissed. This way, he continued, new charges would be processed by way of preliminary hearings, rather than the grand jury.

Predictably, Castro's attorney, Herman Sillas, takes issue with the district attorney. He says the new move will deny an opportunity to the Mexican-American community to hear what an appellate court has to say about the composition of the grand jury.

Retorts Hecht: "We're as anxious as anyone else to learn whether our grand juries are illegally constituted—which we do not think so—but a ruling from the appellate court does not seem to be in sight."

Hecht also pointed out that there is a Sirhan Sirhan appeal in the State Supreme Court involving his claim that Los Angeles grand juries are not representative and that a ruling in that case could clear the air on the matter.[*]

The fact remains, however, that according to the U.S. Commission on Civil Rights, in Los Angeles County, with almost 500,000 eligible Spanish surname residents, only four served as grand jurors during a 12-year period studied.

Sillas also wonders why if Castro is being charged with felonious conspiracy in the school walkouts, no teacher was so charged during the recent teacher's strike.

Hecht answers that in the first place there is some evidence of violence in the East Los Angeles walkouts—which is denied by the participants and that besides, the teachers' strike involved a union. "Union activities have a greater degree of protection under the First Amendment than do other activities," Hecht said.

The point is that whatever one may think of the merits of either side in these cases, grassroot movements such as the school walkouts bring out these important overall issues. And that is what democracy is about.

*Sirhan Sirhan was convicted of murdering Senator Robert Kennedy on the evening of Kennedy's victory in the 1968 California Democratic presidential primary.

Source: "Mexican-American School Walkout Focused on Problem" in Ruben Salazar, *Border Correspondent: Selected Writings, 1955–1970* (Berkeley: University of California Press, 1995). Republished with permission of the University of California Press © 1995; permission conveyed through Copyright Clearance Center, Inc.

## Police Brutality

Police brutality and misconduct have been a cross to bear for the Chicano community and other communities of color to this day. The first document presents a study by the U.S. Commission on Civil Rights with concrete examples that still resonate. In the second document, Rosalío Muñoz, the youthful leader and organizer of the Chicano Moratorium against the Vietnam War, gives a thoughtful and historical synthesis of the toll police brutality has taken on the community. In the third document, Alcohol, Tobacco and Firearms Division (ATF) provocateur Frank Martinez, who actually took over chairmanship of the Moratorium committee from Muñoz, exposes how far law enforcement went to discredit and destabilize the groups it targeted.

# From *Mexican Americans and the Administration of Justice in the Southwest*, 1970

Some of the incidents reported to the Commission had resulted in death. These generally involved resistance to arrest or an attempt to escape from police custody. Mexican-Americans have asserted that the police officers would not have used deadly force against an Anglo under similar circumstances.

One such incident occurred in Stanton, California. According to one of the leaders of the local Mexican-American community, two young men en route home late one night were stopped, questioned, and searched by a police officer. The officer reportedly assigned no reason for his actions but said he was going to take them to jail because they lacked identification. At that point, it was reported, one of the young men, aged 18, started to run away from the officer, whereupon a cruising police car stopped and an officer who saw the youth running fired his revolver, killing the young man. The officer was prosecuted on a charge of involuntary manslaughter, but the case was dismissed after the prosecution presented its case.

A similar incident occurred in Alpine, Texas, in June, 1968. According to reports of local residents, a police officer was chasing Henry Ramos, a 16-year-old Mexican American driving a car, in order to get information about his brother. The officer, it was reported, had a reputation for being rough and abusive and had been accused in the past of harassing Ramos, his brother, and other Mexican-Americans. The chase ended when the boy stopped his car and fled on foot, and the pursuing officer shot him once—fatally. A police investigation resulted in the filing of a charge of murder without malice against the officer and an indictment by the local grand jury.

*Source:* United States Commission on Civil Rights, *Mexican Americans and the Administration of Justice in the Southwest* (Washington, DC: GPO, 1970), 406.

# From *Rosalio Munoz's Letter to the Editor*, 1971

We, of the Chicano Moratorium Committee, are writing to you in response to your plea for some social facts to understand the strained situation between Chicanos and the police. The current conflict between Chicanos and the police is a political confrontation that historically has its roots in the mid-1800s when another police government body—the U.S. Army—forcibly took the land away from the Mexicans in this area. Subsequent brutal acts by border patrol and immigration law enforcement officers frequently leading to reciprocal violent defensive reactions by Mexicans made the situation more acute. The deportation of 312,000 persons of Spanish surname—many American citizens—by immigration law enforcement officials during the Great Depression for political-economic reasons further strained and intensified the anger of people of Mexican descent toward the law and law enforcement.

Denying the Mexican-American population in Los Angeles protection from rioting vigilante servicemen during the 1943 "Zoot Suit" riots, raised further doubts in Mexican Americans as to whom it actually was that the police were there to "protect and serve." Labeling the riots "Zoot Suit" only served to reveal the racist motivations of the press by applying an historically permanent label that implied "the Mexicans did it," thereby simultaneously protecting the servicemen from public ridicule. The Sheriff's department Captain Ayers' "biological basis" racist report to the county grand jury during this period, which stated that people of Mexican descent were biologically prone to criminal behavior, further intensified public racist attitudes towards Mexican Americans, which also had the effect of permitting more aggressive police behavior toward a "biologically crime-prone" population. The report was commended as an "intelligent statement" by LAPD Chief Horral. Subsequently, in 1960, Chief Parker revealed his racist attitudes toward Mexican Americans [absorbed by the LAPD] when he said that Mexican Americans were like "wild Indians from the mountains of Mexico" and that genes had to be considered when discussing the "Mexican problem." Today police have changed the label to "Communism" to discredit legitimate Chicano grievances and elicit public support for police, initiated violence.

It has been a Chicano experience that when he has attempted to protest peacefully against the educational institutions that produce and excessively high Chicano student drop-out rate; against the wealthy Catholic Church that has milked the Chicano of his meager financial resources with no reciprocal benefits; and against the U.S. involvement in the Vietnam war which has resulted in a sever overrepresentation of Chicano deaths (in effect depriving the Chicano community of its future youth resource), his efforts have always been met with police-initiated political violence. In this respect, the police have been given and have adopted a sentry role to protect and serve these institutions that are gradually, socially and psychologically, destroying a class of people along with their rich, proud heritage and tradition. Chicanos, by day and night, are reminded of their low status in society by a sentry helicopter that was not a "called for" service by the Chicano community. The Chicano lives in a totalitarian-like atmosphere within a broader Los Angeles community that is comfortably (with the exception of the black community) functioning as a democracy. Being a population group numbering close to a million in this area, we have no city or county-elected Mexican American political representative to assist us with our problems. Our behavior can only be seen as a normal response to an abnormal condition created by those in political power.

The police brutality that occurs ten to twenty times a month in East Los Angeles again communicates to us our worth to the broader society that does not seem to care. We have not received federal protection against this abuse since the law was initially enacted in 1872. We desperately wish to be part of this society, but your powerful sentry repeatedly sends us away bleeding. We are now directly protesting against the sentry. But it is not only the day-to-day police brutality that we have experienced for numerous decades that gravely concerns us, but rather a far more severe problem that our society is not even aware of, and that is that the police are increasingly becoming more a powerful political force in our increasingly less-free democratic society. The recent Skolnic Report to the National Commission on the Causes and Prevention of Violence warned that "the ranks of law enforcement have become an ultraconservative social force which shrilly protest positive change." The report also concluded that the increasing police militancy is hostile to the aspirations of dissident groups in society and that the police view protesters as a danger to our American political system. Although this is a national report, the situation is identical in Los Angeles as confirmed not only by our experience, but by the recent UCLA report of the May 5,1970, student-police confrontation, which stated that "police attack was discriminatory, focusing on minority group members and long hairs."

Rather than calling off our protest, and returning to a life of fear under police totalitarian aggression we gave to continue to protest for purposes of survival. If Chicanos lose their right to protest in society because of police violence, you likewise are losing your freedom in America. In this respect, our insistence on the right to protest guarantees the right of all people in America to protest. If we allow police violence to intimidate us, it is really the broader society that is victimized. (375–376)

Source: Rosalio Muñoz, cochair of the Chicano Moratorium Committee. Edited by the Los Angeles Times before being published on January 23, 1971. Printed with permission of the Brown Berets.

# From *Chicano Leader Tells of Starting Violence to Justify Arrests*, 1972

Another police informer surfaced in the Los Angeles area last Monday under the auspices of the Citizens' Research and Investigating Committee (CRIC), this time with the warning to still active informants that, "It does not pay to be an informer because when they no longer need you, they'll frame you."

These words were spoken by Eustacio (Frank) Martinez at the end of a press conference at the Los Angeles Press Club, where he revealed that for two years he had worked as police informer among Chicano activists in Texas and California.

Martinez, 23, told the assembled newsmen that he had been an informer and agent provocateur for the Alcohol, Tobacco and Firearms Enforcement Division of the U.S. Treasury Department (ATF) and under instructions from his supervisors had committed illegal acts which allowed the police to make arrests and raid headquarters of the Chicano Moratorium Committee.

Martinez, repeating taped statements he had previously given CRIC investigators, said that following his arrest for possession of an illegal weapon in Houston, Texas, in July of 1969, he was contacted by one "Tito Garcia," who identified himself as an agent for ATF. Garcia stated that Martinez would not be charged for the Federal Firearms violation if he would work as an informant and agent provocateur for that agency. Martinez, upon his agreed release from jail, was given and carried out the assignments of infiltrating the Mexican-American Youth Organization (MAYO) and the Brown Berets in Houston and Kingsville, Texas; provided intelligence on both groups and their members; and committed acts of provocation and violence in his role as militant Chicano leader.

During this period from September, 1969, to October, 1970, Martinez participated in a protest march in Alice, Texas, designed to bring attention to the educational problems of Chicanos and attempted disruption by jumping on a car and trying to cave its top in. He also, along with "Tito Garcia," attempted to set up a purchase of guns from members of the local MAYO.

During this same period he burned a cross in front of the home of Katie Brooks, a Vista worker in Houston, and later burned her house down. During high school demonstrations in Houston, he also crossed the police line in an attempt to create violence against MAYO instructions.

After purchasing some explosives while he was a Brown Beret organizer he somehow blew his cover and was suspected of being an informer. At this point (October, 1970), he was sent to Los Angeles by the Alcohol, Tobacco, and Firearms Division along with "Tito Garcia," who remained his contact until January, 1971, when Martinez was introduced to ATF Agents Fernando Ramos and Jim Riggs.

Once in Los Angeles, Martinez began spreading rumors against Rosalio Munoz, then Chairman of the Chicano Moratorium Committee. He accused Munoz of being too soft, "not militant enough, and not going all the way, as he should." This resulted in the ouster of Munoz which allowed Martinez to become Chairman of the Moratorium Committee himself in November, 1970. He continued as Chairman until March, 1971, when he took a trip back to Texas.

During his period of leadership in the Moratorium Committee, Martinez said that he continually advocated the use of illegal weapons and violent tactics. During a picket line at the Hollenbeck Police Station, Martinez interfered with a police officer who was ticketing the car of a female demonstrator. This resulted in the arrest of both Martinez and the woman. He stole letters and other documents from the Chicano Moratorium office and paraded in front of the office with a shotgun in order to provoke a raid, which took place that same day.

. . .

Upon returning to Los Angeles, Martinez was then given instructions by ATF agents Riggs and Ramos to infiltrate a Chicano organization, La Casa de Carnalismo. At this time Martinez was given a membership list and shown photographs by agents Riggs and Ramos to help him identify "leading militants" and possible members of the Chicano Liberation Front (CLF). Martinez was told that CLF was responsible for all the bombings in East Los Angeles, that La Casa de Carnalismo was the overground name for CLF, and that if it were necessary for Martinez to carry out bombings himself, he should do so and ATF would supply the necessary explosives.

Martinez then stated that he made contact with La Casa on various occasions in late June and early July of 1971, trying to find out where CLF was getting its explosives. He states that he reported back to Riggs and Ramos that he never heard mention of CLF at La Casa, he never discussed or heard discussed acts of violence by La Casa members, and that the program of La Casa was immigration counselling, English classes for Chicanos, self-defense classes and the dispensing of food to needy families. The main concern of La Casa, in fact, was the elimination of illegal narcotics, especially heroin and barbiturates from the Chicano community.

At that time, Martinez states, he was told that his "information was a bunch of bullshit" and that "we are going to close that organization down by any means necessary." Riggs and Ramos also told Martinez that his job was infiltration and order taking and they would worry about the rest.

. . .

In September, 1971, Martinez made a court appearance concerning charges arising out of demonstrating on August, 1971, the anniversary of the "Chicano Moratorium Riots." Martinez was charged with inciting to riot and interference with a police officer. Because he had incurred those charges under ATF orders, he had been promised protection from prosecution. However, Martinez states that Riggs appeared and attempted to force Martinez to plead guilty, with the intention of sending him back to Texas. When a newsman asked Martinez why he had decided to publicly tell his story at this time, Martinez replied, "For the simple reason that I was beginning to be aware that our people were being railroaded, and for another thing, I was being sold out. I had good intentions of working for the government. I believed in it. When I began to see how corrupt the government was in destroying my people, I couldn't see it anymore.

*Source:* Art Kunkin, *Los Angeles Free Press*, February 2–10, 1972. Vol. 9, No. 5 (Issue 394), 1–3.

## The Chicano Moratorium & *Más Protestas*

Protests by Chicano groups battled racism and discrimination on a number of fronts and hinted at the potential of a waking giant. Even conservative Mexican American groups that had previously been docile and little prone to activism were becoming aggressive. The first document explains the position of the Mexican American delegates from six states in the Southwest who pulled out of a federal Equal Employment Opportunities Commission convention. The second document is a manifesto that presents Chicanos' positions on and feelings about the Vietnam War, which led to the moratorium protests and riots. The final document demonstrates that even passive Mexican American Catholics found the courage to protest marginalization and neglect from their church. Catolicos por La Raza's Christmas Eve protest at St. Basil's is, after all, the riot that sets the tone for *Revolt* from that opening chapter:

"Three hundred Chicanos have gathered in front of St. Basil's Roman Catholic Church. Three hundred brown-eyed children of the sun have come to drive the money-changers out of the riches temple in Los Angeles" (11).

## From *Walkout in Albuquerque*, 1966

All 59 Mexican-American delegates representing six Southwestern states walked out on a federal Equal Employment Opportunity Commission conference here today, after charging that the Commission is indifferent to Mexican-American needs and guilty of discrimination in its own hiring practices.

The walkout took place less than an hour after the scheduled all-day conference began.

. . .

The group was also critical of the fact that only one commissioner, Richard A. Graham, attended the long-publicized conference—and that he came without any background in Mexican-American employment problems.

He was presented with eight resolutions drawn up by the delegates expressing their dissatisfaction. The resolution were directed to President Johnson who, according to Pena, was wired a copy. The resolution statement read:

We, the delegates representing Mexican-American organizations from throughout the Pacific Southwestern states, realize that further participation in this conference—under conditions imposed upon us by the federal Equal Employment Opportunity Commission—will be valueless.

Through its actions both here and in Washington, D.C. the Commission has shown a total lack of interest and understanding of the problems facing our nation's six million Mexican-Americans.

We feel that the Commission has been insincere in its relations with the Mexican-American community.

Rather than continuing to deal with this body, as it is presently constituted, we are making the following appeal to the President of the United States, Lyndon B. Johnson, so that our community may share in the prosperity which should be part of our American heritage.

To President Johnson, we submit the following resolutions (all delegates were urged to wire President Johnson asking him to name a Mexican-American to the Commission):

1. That at least one Mexican-American, with full understanding of the unique employment problems of Americas second-largest minority, be appointed to the five-member Equal Employment Opportunity Commission.
2. That staff hiring practices of the EEOC—an organization which should serve as a model for all of our nation's employers, be investigated and changed to eliminate current ethnic imbalances which work against the Mexican-American.
3. That the commission send knowledgeable representatives to any future conferences involving federal agencies and the Mexican-American community.
4. That regional offices of the EEOC be relocated into areas where employment discrimination is most severe.
5. That the entire program of the EEOC be reoriented, and new procedures be established to reach the Mexican-American community.
6. That the Mexican-American be allowed full participation in the upcoming June White House Conference on Civil Rights, and to all other civil rights programs and activities engaged in or sponsored by the federal government.
7. That the EEOC take immediate steps against some 800 major national companies in the Pacific Southwest which have more than 600,000 employees on their payrolls, yet hire no Mexican-Americans.
8. That the hiring practices of all governmental agencies be reviewed and that affirmative action be taken to rectify present imbalances against Mexican-Americans and all other ethnic minorities. (211–214)

*Source: Carta Editorial*, Vol. 3, No. 12, April 8, 1966.

# From *Mexican Americans Protest the Vietnam War*, 1970

The Congress of Mexican American Unity, an affiliation of more than 300 diverse organizations in Los Angeles, wishes to inform you of its opposition to escalation of the Vietnam War. The overwhelming majority of our people can no longer remain silent in the face of the Cambodian invasion.

This political and moral tragedy can only bring more sorrow to the Mexican American community who already bear the heavy burden of the Vietnam War, by the disproportionate sacrifice of their youth.

Social progress in our barrios, Mr. President depends largely on our people's faith in the honesty and goodwill of our elected leaders, such as you. Your action, which is contrary to your stated commitment to peace and social progress in the ghettos, has led us to question that faith. . .

We hope and pray that you will alter your course and give more consideration to national issues that are tearing our country apart; the hope and aspirations of our people are dependent on it.

. . . the National Chicano Moratorium will convene to show the world that the Chicano will no longer fight against their brothers in far off lands and that the Chicano recognizes that the fight is here at home against a government that oppresses and jails its poor people and as we know, even kills them. . .

The Chicano will take to the streets Saturday to protest U.S. aggression throughout the world: and (1) the war in Vietnam, (2) the high rate of Chicano casualties, (3) the attitude the U.S. has as the world's policeman, using our brothers to die for their interest, (4) the police aggression used in our own barrios, and (5) the United States' imperialistic position throughout the world.

We Chicanos have come to a realization the Vietnam War is the ultimate weapon of genocide of nonwhite peoples. . . . . The random genocide in the barrio, *campo* [fields] and ghettos is escalated to a calculated cold-blooded policy to enslave the Vietnamese people and rape their land of its resources. It is a war of example to other third world colonies both outside and inside the borders of the United States that they dare not resist or they will be napalmed or gunned down. (374)

*Source: Mexican American Sun*, May 14, 1970.

# From *Catolicos por La Raza*, 1970

We wish to share with you the feelings which gave rise to Catolicos por La Raza. As Mexican-Americans and as Catholics you have a right to know.

Members of Catolicos por La Raza (CPLR) are Catholics. We have gone to Catholic schools and understand the Catholic tradition. Because of our Catholic training we know that Christ, the founder of Catholicism was a genuinely poor man. We know that he was born in a manger because His compatriots refused Him better housing. We know that He not only washed and kissed the feet of the poor (Mary Magdalen) but did all in His power to feed and educate the poor. We also know that one day He rode through Jerusalem on a jackass and was laughed at, spat upon, and ridiculed. We remember, from Catholic education, that Christ, our hero, did not have to identify with the poor but chose to do so. We also were taught that one day Christ went to the established church, a church which identified with the rich people, with people who were never ridiculed or laughed at or spat upon, and He took a whip and used it upon the money-changers of His day who, in the name of religion, would dare to gather money from the poor. And, finally, we know, as all Christians know, His love for the poor was so great that He chose to die for poor people.

We know these things because our Catholic education has taught us that these were the things Christ did, Christ who founded the Catholic Church. And we know further that if you or I claim to be Christian we have the duty to not only love the poor but to be as Christlike as possible.

It is these feelings within us, as members of Catolicos por La Raza, which led us to look at our Catholic Church as it presently exists: a Church which, for example in Los Angeles, would dare to build a $3,500,000 church on Wilshire Boulevard when you and we know that because of our poverty our average education is 8.6 years and many, too many of our people, live in projects. How many churches, let alone million-dollar churches, did Christ build? We looked further and found that, although as a matter of faith all of us are members of the Catholic Church, nonetheless no Chicanos are able to participate in decisions within the Church, which are not of purely religious nature. Would you have voted for a million-dollar Church?

So many other considerations led to the creation of Catolicos por La Raza. We do not have the time or the money to print them all. But we do ask you to remember, as Mexican-Americans, as Catolicos, as Chicanos, that as members of the Catholic Church, it is our fault if the Catholic Church in the Southwest is no longer a Church of blood, a Church of struggle, a Church of sacrifice. It is our fault because we have not raised our voices as Catholics and as poor people for the love of Christ. We can't love our people without demanding better housing, education, health, and so many other needs we share in common.

In a word, we are demanding that the Catholic Church practice what it preaches. Remember Padre Hidalgo. And remember than the history of our people is the history of the Catholic Church in the Americas. We must return the Church to the poor. **Or did Christ die in vain?** (391–392)

*Source: La Raza, February 1970.*

## La Raza Unida Party

The Brown Buffalo—and Oscar Z. Acosta himself—memorably runs for sheriff on the LRUP ticket. At the time, LRUP presented the best opportunity for Chicanos to unite and bring their influence to bear in electoral politics in order to effect change. The first document presents LRUP's platform in Colorado where it is evident that the party's goal is the creation of a Chicano nation. In contrast, the platform for the LRUP in Texas does not share that extreme goal; the second document lays out its advocacy for radical changes nonetheless. For example, LRUP Texas claimed that the natural resources should belong to the people of the state, pointed out the need to rectify the judicial system's double standard, called for a redistribution of wealth, and called for the removal of economic sanctions against Cuba. The third document is a wicked excerpt from Texas LRUP party leader José Angel Gutiérrez's parody of a manual, an acerbic denunciation of the many ways the "Gringo" powers stifle and frustrate Chicano activism.

# From *Colorado Platform*. La Raza Unida Party, 1972

EDUCATION: "We resolve that schools be warm and inviting facilities and not similar to jails in any way. . . .

"We resolve that all teachers live within walking distance of the schools. We demand that from kindergarten through college, Spanish be the first language and English the second language and the text books be rewritten to emphasize the heritage and contributions of the Mexican-American or Indio-Hispano in the building of the Southwest. We also demand the teaching of the contributions and history of other minorities which have also helped build this country. We also feel that each neighborhood school complex should have its own school board made up of members who live in the community the school serves."

ECONOMIC OPPORTUNITIES: "We resolve that the businesses serving our community be owned by that community. Seed money is required to start cooperative grocery stores, gas stations, furniture stores, etc. Instead of our people working in bit factories across the city, we want training and low interest loans to set up small industries in our communities. These industries would be co-ops with the profits staying in the community."

AGRICULTURAL REFORMS: "We resolve that not only the land which is our ancestral right be given back to those pueblos with restitution given for mineral, natural resources, grazing and timber used.

"We resolve compensation for taxes, legal costs, etc. which pueblos and heirs spent trying to save their land."

. . .

LAW ENFORCEMENT: "We resolve an immediate investigation of the records of all prisoners to correct the legal errors, or detect the prejudice which operated in those court proceedings, causing their convictions or extra heavy sentencing. As these cases are found, we demand that the federal government reimburse those prisoners for loss of time and money.

"We resolve immediate suspension of officers suspected of police brutality until a full hearing is held in the neighborhood of the event.

"We resolve suspension of the city-wide juvenile court system and the creation instead of a neighborhood community court to deal with allegations of crime. In addition, instead of prowl-car precinct system, we want to gradually install a neighborhood protection system where residents are hired for every few families to assist and safeguard in matters of community safety or possible crime.

FARM LABOR: "We resolve that the farm laborers be represented on the NLRB. They must receive the benefits of Social Security and unemployment compensation."

. . .

LAND REFORM: "A complete re-evaluation of the Homestead Act to provide people ownership of the natural resources that abound in this country. Birthright should not only place responsibility on the individual but grant him ownership in the land that he dies for."

REDISTRIBUTION OF THE WEALTH: "That all citizens of this country share in the wealth of this nation by institution of economic reforms that would provide for all people and that welfare in this form of subsidies in taxes and payoffs to corporate owners be reverted to the people who in reality are the foundation of the economy and the tax base for this society."

WAR IN VIETNAM: "We resolve that"

(1)    Draft boards representative of the population.
(2)    That members of the draft boards be thirty-five (35) years of younger and that these draft boards be appointed every four years concurrent with the election for Governor.
(3)    That this war is unjust and only a form of genocide that has been used against La Raza to eliminate our natural resource—our youth! (9,000 deaths, 20 pct. Of the war deaths, 47,000 total killed.) The government's war machine has used the concepts of "Machismo" against La Raza and has succeeded in making La Raza one of the most decorated if not the most decorated minority in the country.

(4)    We resolve and do condemn the war in Southeast Asia. This unde-
clared police action that has expanded into this present war situation is unjust and has been unjust from its inception.

June 20, 1970. Alamosa, Colorado
Adopted at the third nominating convention of La Raza Unida Party.

*Source:* Christine Marín, *A Spokesman of the Mexican American Movement: Rodolfo "Corky" Gonzales and the Fight for Chicano Liberation, 1966–1972* (San Francisco, CA: R and E Research Associates, Inc., 1977), 38. Reprinted with permission from Christine Marín.

# From *Texas Raza Unida Party. Political Action Program for the '70s*, 1972

## *Raza Unida Party*

### *Preamble*

La Raza, recognizing the need to replace the existing system with a human-
istic alternative which shall maintain equal representation of all people;

And, recognizing the need to create a government which serves the needs of individual communities, yet is beneficial to the general populace;

And, recognizing the need to create a political movement dedicated to ending the causes of poverty, misery and injustice so that future generations can live a life free from exploitation;

And, recognizing the need to abolish racist practices within the exist-
ing social, educational, economic and political system so that physical and cultural genocidal practices against minorities will be discontinued;

Therefore resolves, to these ends, because we are the people who have been made aware of the needs of the many through our suffering, who have learned the significance of *carnalismo*, the strength of *la familia* and the importance of people working together; and recognizing the natural right of all peoples to preserve their self-identity and to formulate their own destiny.

To establish Raza Unida Party, with courage and love in our hearts, a firm commitment to mankind, and with peace in our minds.

### *Education*

... Therefore, Raza Unida Party, affirming that the problem in the educational system is one primarily of money and value-orientations, resolves to:

1.    Make the method of financing public education a function of the wealth of the entire state rather than the relative wealth of districts or economic classes. The property tax must be abolished.

The natural resources of the State of Texas must be claimed by the people of Texas; then, corporations wishing to utilize or exploit a public resource would be required to obtain a lease and deposit a portion of their earnings into a State Education Fund.

2. Increase the level of spending for education to upgrade the entire educational system to one of excellence.

3. Establish a separate fund, maintained by a portion of the revenues from a state income tax, to support additional educational programs for low-income and minority groups.

## Politics

Chicanos in Texas have been powerless since Santana was defeated at San Jacinto in 1836. This lack of power affects the lives of Chicanos as well as those who have also remained powerless socially, culturally, economically, educationally and politically. Subsequently, most of the problems facing the people are a direct result of this powerlessness. The solution, then, is obvious. Those who are powerless need to get power if we are to resolve our problem.

An analysis of the system which governs us and how it functions always brings us to the same point. Those who have power can make things happen and those who do not are helpless. Then, anyone who want to change the status-quo must have clear understanding of the power relationships in this society. These relationships are always the same under the political system which governs us. Those who have the most money are the most powerful and the ones who control the institutions or the top administrators who run these institutions. Further, we must understand that the rich always use their money to perpetuate themselves in power. Clearly, anyone who wants to transfer power with the least obstacles and least delays must get the favor of the rich. Obviously, this can only be done by selling-out to the power wielders.

. . .

Again, history has shown us that the Democratic and Republican Parties have never had (and never will have) the interest or desire to serve the needs of the Chicano community. Clearly, they have shown that all they want to is use us for their benefit only. Constantly, they refused to respond to the demands of the Chicano community. Year after year, these two parties have conspired, through their selfish and hypocritical politicians to keep La Raza in chains, economically and politically. Their false prophets have always given us nothing but unfulfilled promises. Clearly, these are not the parties which will bring social change to improve the Chicano living conditions. Clearly, if La Raza is to improve socially, economically and politically, we cannot depend on those two parties. La Raza must formulate its own political strategy, independent of the Democrats and the Republicans. Chicanos need and must have our own independent political party—Raza Unida Party.

## *Economics*

. . .

Raza Unida Party resolves to:

1. Reduce the economic advantage of the very rich by ending the regressive nature of taxes.
2. Restore, by a combination of measures, the element of competition to the economy, i.e., breaking up monopolies and trusts by vigorous anti-trust activity, instituting public corporations in competition with the private sector, and supporting and sponsoring community cooperative ventures.
3. Increase the flow of transfer payments to the poor for the purpose of starting what the economic system has not been able to do—distribute the wealth on a more equitable basis.

## *Justice*

Since the early 1960's, the United States Commission on Civil Rights has been documenting the biased treatment received by minorities within the judicial system and law enforcement agencies of the State of Texas. Discriminatory treatment has been recorded, from verbal abuse to violent treatment, from unwarranted arrests to improper use of bail, from under-representation in law enforcement agencies and juries to lack of serious inquiry into these allegations at all levels of government. . . . The Commission found that this had brought about an attitude of mistrust, fear and hostility on the part of the Chicano and Black communities toward the agencies of law enforcement. . .

By providing most Anglo communities with law and order and inadequately serving the minority communities, the judicial system has succeeded in creating a double standard. The creation of this double standard has ultimately caused a failure within the judicial system and law enforcement agencies to provide equal protection under the law.

. . .

Under International Affairs:

Recognizing the bond of suffering and the consequent common struggle that unites all oppressed peoples throughout the world, and recognizing the need for a more just redistribution of the wealth, Raza Unida Party offers the following resolutions as indications of their solidarity with all those people opposing the class and power elites:

1.  That the U.S. no longer provide military or economic intervention in the national schemes of other countries, since and intervention is used by those who rule to suppress their own people and by demagogues to suppress neighboring peoples;
2.  That U.S. forces in Europe be cut by 2/3 (66%) since the outbreak of a conventional war on that continent is extremely unlikely;
3.  That the Central Intelligence Agency (CIA) discontinue activities in other nations which aid the U.S. businessmen and corporations in maintaining puppet governments, since such efforts are always at the expense of the working people;
4.  That a systematic withdrawal of all U.S. forces from all of Indochina be initiated immediately, thereby allowing the peoples of the area self/determination.
5.  That the U.S. recognize and support the efforts of the New State of Bangladesh as a necessary means . . .
6.  That the U.S. remove embargos and economic sanctions on Cuba and any other country, thus recognizing the right of each nation to choose its own form of government.

*Source:* Raza Unida Party Platform, Houston, Texas, 1972. Raza Unida Party Records, 1969–1979, Nettie Lee Benson Latin American Collection, University of Texas Libraries, the University of Texas at Austin.

# From *A Gringo Manual on How to Handle Mexicans*, 1974

## Preface

This little book is intended for Chicanos only, but I am sure it will fall into the clutches of the enemy from time to time. They will certainly profit from it. However, Chicanos should profit even more.

These pages do not exhaust the subject of all the devious, treacherous, hypocritical gringo machinations used against our Raza. But there is a good collection here. Chicanos who know the gringo tricks won't be fooled by them anymore. That's why we are in control of Cristal.

. . .

I present this beginning list of tricks with one end in view. I want Chicanos to employ this knowledge systematically against the gringo.

Granted, the years of oppression will not be ended with this book—or any book. I realize that books in themselves do not end oppression. . . . This book is a limited manual on how to deal with a racist, imperialist, colonialized society of white people.

Chicanos cannot by theory alone; we must pick up tools of our liberation. This book is a tool. (73–75)

## Law and Order Category

### TRICK NUMBER 8: BROWN PIGS

Chicanos have long complained about police brutality. The Texas Rangers, the migra, the local pigs are almost always lily-white. When Chicanos protest the brutality and discrimination of the pigs, invariably someone will demand more Chicanos on the police force. Bad mistake.

Chicanos get what they want. Brown pigs must be tougher and meaner than gringos in beating other Chicanos. Now even the *rinches* have a few Chicanos on board.

## Political Category

### TRICK NUMBER 39: PROVE YOUR CITIZENSHIP

You walk into the polling place. You are going to vote. You announce your name and address. The election judge does not welcome you or say hello before showing you to the booth. He asks you to prove your citizenship.

Or, you are walking down the street and you get deported to México because it is pretty clear you are a Mexican. Just like that. Just because you can't prove your citizenship.

I'll bet you ten-to-one that the average American at any given time on any given day would be hard pressed to prove his citizenship for the main reason that the average American doesn't carry his birth certificate around with him.

Chicanos in this part of the country are selectively picked up and asked to produce their citizenship proof on the spot, then and there, because where we live is close to México. However, I notice that Canadians don't have that kind of trouble living in Buffalo, New York. Canadians look like average gringos.

Puerto Ricans don't have that kind of trouble on the East Coast, either, because Puerto Rico is part of the United States. But if a Puerto Rican comes down here to South Texas, and he just lands in San Antonio, for instance, he is going to be picked up sooner or later because now, with his brown skin and his talking Spanish and all, he is going to look like a Mexican.

The trick is to keep that line clear. Even native-born Americans of Mexican descent are very good Americans and are always suspect. (95)

*Source:* José Angel Gutiérrez, *A Gringo Manual on How to Handle Mexicans*, Second edition, revised and expanded (Houston, TX: Arte Público Press, 2001), 73–75, 95. Reprinted with permission from Arte Público Press.

## Notes

1. This dedication is at variance with Acosta's narrator Buffalo Brown's persona as the caricature of a macho sexist pig. I think of it as an apologia for the portrayal of the female characters to come and a hint that Acosta appreciated Chicanas' contributions to the movement.
2. Huitzilopochtli was the Aztec god of war.
3. The Walk Outs are also called Blow Outs. The term is variously spelled with or without a hyphen and as one word or two.
4. This scene will resonate with modern readers familiar with the 2015 Sandra Bland case: an African American woman arrested on a minor traffic stop who died in a Texas jail, an alleged suicide according to authorities although her family and friends contest that conclusion.
5. Hunter S. Thompson, Introduction to *The Revolt of the Cockroach People*, p. 6.
6. For Acosta, it damaged his standing with the *vatos locos*; he received death threats from Chicano militants for collaborating with the *gabacho* gonzo journalist and after his own drug bust was virtually abandoned by his former allies—the *vatos* he struggled with and went to jail for.

## Suggested Readings

Acosta, Oscar Zeta. *The Autobiography of a Brown Buffalo.* New York: Vintage Press, 1989.

Baca, Hernan. "The Chicano Moratorium August 29, 1970. Still Remembered after 35 Years." *La Prensa San Diego*, August 26, 2005. http://laprensa-sandiego.org/archieve/august26–05/chicano.htm. Retrieved March 19, 2016.

Burciaga, José Antonio. *Drink Cultura: Chicanismo.* Santa Barbara, CA: Joshua Odell Editions, 1993.

Gómez Quiñones, Juan. *Chicano Politics: Reality & Promise 1940–1990.* Albuquerque, NM: University of New Mexico Press, 1990.

Gonzalez, Juan and Joseph Torres. *News for All the People: The Epic Story of Race and the American Media.* New York: Verso, 2011.

Gutiérrez, José Angel. *A Gringo Manual on How to Handle Mexicans.* Houston, TX: Arte Público Press, 2001.

Hames-García, Michael. "Dr. Gonzo's Carnival: The Testimonial Satires of Oscar Zeta Acosta" *American Literature* 72, no. 3 (September 2000).

Haney López, Ian F. *Racism on Trial: The Chicano Fight for Justice.* Cambridge, MA: Harvard University Press, 2003.

Lee, A. Robert. "*Chicanismo's* Beat Outrider? The Texts and Contexts of Oscar Zeta Acosta." *College Literature* 27 no. 1 (Winter 2000): 158–176.

Marín, Christine. *A Spokesman for the Mexican American Movement.* San Francisco: R and E Research Associates, 1977.

Mendoza, Louis. "On Buffaloes, Body Snatching, and Bandidismo: Ilan Stavans's Appropriation of Oscar Acosta and the Chicano Experience," *Bilingual Review* 26, no. 1 (January–April 2001/2002): 79–86.

Moore, Burton and Andrea Alessandra Cabello, eds. *Love and Riot: Oscar Zeta Acosta and the Great Mexican American Revolt.* Mountain View, CA: Floricanto Press, 2003.

Muñoz, Carlos, Jr. *Youth, Identity, Power: The Chicano Movement.* New York: Verso, 1989.

Olmos, Edward James, dir. *Walkout.* HBO Video, 2006.

Rodríguez, Phillip, dir. *Ruben Salazar: Man in the Middle.* PBS Home Video, 2014.

Rosales, F. Arturo. *Testimonio: A Documentary History of the Mexican American Struggle for Civil Rights.* Houston, TX: Arte Público Press, 2000.

Schryer, Stephen, "Cockroach Dreams: Oscar Zeta Acosta, Legal Services, and the Great Society Coalition" *Twentieth-Century Literature* 60, no. 4 (Winter 2014): 455–480.

Smethurst, James. "The Figure of the *Vato Loco* and the Representation of Ethnicity in the Narrative of Oscar Z. Acosta." *MELUS* 20, no. 2 (Summer 1995): 120–132.

Stavans, Ilan, ed. *Oscar "Zeta" Acosta: The Uncollected Works.* Houston, TX: Arte Público Press, 1996.

Thompson, Hunter S. *Fear and Loathing at Rolling Stone: The Essential Writing of Hunter S. Thompson.* New York: Simon & Schuster, 2011.

Thompson, Hunter S. *Fear and Loathing in America: The Brutal Odyssey of an Outlaw Journalist.* London, England: Bloomsbury Publishing, 2000.

Thompson, Hunter S. *Fear and Loathing in Las Vegas and Other American Stories.* New York: Modern Library, 1996.

Tobar, Hector. "Finally, Transparency in the Ruben Salazar case." *Los Angeles Times*, August 5, 2011. http://articles.latimes.com/2011/aug/05/local/la-me-0805-tobar-20110805. Retrieved March 19, 2016.

Wright, Greg. "The Literary, Political, and Legal Strategies of Oscar Zeta Acosta and Hunter S. Thompson: Intertextuality, Ambiguity, and (Naturally) Fear and Loathing." *The Journal of Popular Culture* 43, no. 3 (2010): 622–643.

**4**

# *The House on Mango Street* **(1984)**

*We are continuing in the direction of honoring others' ways, of sharing knowl-edge and personal power through writing (art) and activism, of injecting into our cultures new ways, feminist ways, mestiza ways.*
—Gloria Anzaldúa, *Making Face, Making Soul*, xxvii

*Chicana feminism originates in the community and on the streets as political activism to end the oppression of women. This political movement is insep-arable from the historical experience of Chicanos in this country since 1848, an experience marked by economic exploitation as a class and sys-tematic racial, social and linguistic discrimination designed to keep Chi-canos at the bottom as a reserve pool of cheap labor.*
—Yvonne Yarbro-Bejarano, "Chicana Literature from a
Chicana Feminist Perspective," in *Chicana Creativity
and Criticism*, 213

*La mujer luchando/El mundo transformando = Women in struggle transform
the world*
—Fuerza Unida Union motto cited by Vicki L. Ruiz
in *From Out of the Shadows*, 151

# SYNOPSIS

Sandra Cisneros dedicated her slim novel *The House on Mango Street* "A las mujeres/To the women," a hint that women may be central to the theme of this book. Eleven-year-old narrator Esperanza leads us through 44 vignettes, ranging in length from one short paragraph to four pages, vividly portraying the narrow range of options available to this sensitive, clear-eyed Chicana.[1] Esperanza's stories are prompted by the family's move into a house of their own after being accustomed to moving frequently and at the mercy of landlords' whims. The new house falls far short of Esperanza's ideal, however: "It's small and red with tight steps in front and windows so small you'd think they were holding their breath. Bricks are crumbling in places, and the front door is so swollen you have to push hard to get in" (4). She hints at the marginal status of the new neighborhood by describing how people move out once *our* kind of people start moving in: "they'll just have to move a little farther north from Mango Street, a little farther away every time people like us keep moving in (13)"; those from outside the barrio are afraid when they find themselves in Esperanza's new barrio: "Those who don't know any better come into our neighborhood scared. They think we're dangerous. They think we will attack them with shiny knives."

Esperanza's desire for a "real" house was born when she saw her old apartment on Loomis through the judgmental eyes of a nun from her school—"you live *there*? The way she said it made me feel like nothing" (5). Those eyes put her in a place with a label that, even at that young age, Esperanza knew would be a struggle for her to overcome. Instead, Esperanza yearns for "a house quiet as snow, a space for myself to go, clean as paper before the poem" (108). She intuits her need for a space that will provide her the freedom to become an artist much like Shakespeare's sister in Virginia Woolf's classic essay, "A Room of One's Own." She understands that home for most women in her Mango Street barrio is a confining space for the women who "sit their sadness on an elbow" (11). Beginning with her own wild grandmother who "wouldn't marry. Until my great-grandfather threw a sack over her head and carried her off. Just like that, as if she were a fancy chandelier" (11), to Rapunzel-like Rafaela who "gets locked indoors . . . since she is too beautiful to look at" (79) and asks the children to send her coconut and papaya juice "in a paper shopping bag she lets down with a clothesline" (80), to Sally, Esperanza's young friend who has run away to be married to escape her abusive father only to end up with an abusive husband who "won't let her talk on the telephone. And he doesn't let her look out the window. . . . She sits at home because she is afraid to go outside without his permission" (102).

In Esperanza's barrio, Louie's cousin Marin represents Doña Marina, the archetypal figure from Mexican history. Like her, Marin is sent away from her home—Puerto Rico in Marin's case—abandoned and virtually imprisoned. Her boyfriend left her with Louie's family and she can't leave the house, "She can't come out—gotta baby-sit with Louie's sisters" (23). She "is older and knows a lot of things" (27) like Doña Marina. Esperanza likes and admires Marin but rejects her as a role model since Marin will always be "waiting for a car to stop, a star to fall, someone to change her life" (27) rather than change her own life as Esperanza aims to do. Marin is passive, a sexual object who defines herself by the boys' view of her as she tells Esperanza, "What matters . . . is for the boys to see us and for us to see them" (27).

Instead of accepting the fate of a captive like the women in her barrio, Esperanza hopes to fashion an alternative future for all of them. She instinctively follows the path of fierce Chicana leaders throughout history whose priority was empowerment for the whole community. Esperanza's own strength and the support she enjoys from family, friends and neighbors will provide the tools she needs to make this happen. She embraces her bicultural status—she is a Chicana and the syntax in these poetic vignettes, while written in English, is Spanish. Her name Esperanza means "hope" in English; it is the name she shares with the captive wild woman, her grandmother. She appreciates the beauty and legacy of her name—"made out of a softer something, like silver" but chafes at the English pronunciation and the marginalization it implies—"at school they say my name funny as if the syllables were made out of tin and hurt the roof of your mouth" (11). She would create a name that is something completely new and unique, not linked to any cultural tradition, expectations, or abducted women— "Zeze the X will do" (11) in order to free her from preconceptions from either side. Even though she knows that Mexicans "don't like their women strong" (10), she conducts her "own quiet war. Simple . . . the one who leaves the table like a man, without putting back the chair or picking up the plate" (88–89).

It is the support of family and other women that make Esperanza's triumph possible—her mother, after all, must be the one to pick up her dirty dishes. It is her mother who encourages her to read, to write, and to study, her mother who lives with her own frustrated ambitions—"She borrows opera records from the public library and sings with velvety lungs powerful as morning glories" (90–91). Esperanza's Aunt Lupe and her abused neighbor Minerva give their support by listening to her poems and encouraging her to keep writing—"It will keep you free" (61).

Near the end of the novel, Esperanza is drawn to three strange sisters who visit the barrio to attend a wake for a baby. The sisters look her over, and as in a fairy tale, they tell Esperanza that she will leave Mango Street but that she must come back. Her personal growth and success will bring change and hope to the other women in the community: "I have gone away to come back. For the ones I left behind. For the ones who cannot out" (110); her final statement brings *The House on Mango Street* full circle back to the dedication *A las mujeres*/To the women. Esperanza after all, means hope.

## HISTORICAL BACKGROUND: *THE HOUSE ON MANGO STREET*. CHICANAS: WOMEN AND THE CHICANO MOVEMENT

Throughout the Chicano movement, Chicanas took part in the struggle alongside their Chicano brothers and comrades at every level while suffering double and triple discrimination—from their status as Chicanas, as women, and/or as working class. These women were caught crossways between two movements, forced to examine their priorities, and their priorities were often questioned: Whose side are you on? The Chicano movement or women's liberation?

Chicanas who dedicated their passion, time, and efforts to the Chicano movement were expected to perform the most lowly, menial, "female" tasks, that is, secretarial work, food preparation, and cleanup. In the Chicano family, they fulfilled the traditional role of submissive and fertile wife, mother of as many children as God might bless the union with. When Chicanas demanded equal treatment and respect for their choices and opinions, they were accused of being sell-outs/*vendidas* or *agringadas* (acting like gringas/white women) or even *Malinchistas*. Many Chicanas were also frustrated and hurt by the Chicano men's double standard who, when working with non-Chicanas, treated them as equals, deferred to them, and often chose them as romantic partners. In historian Rodolfo Acuña's words, Chicanas "were frustrated by the lack of political maturity of many Chicanos in recognizing the equal participation of women" (Acuña 394).

Vicki L. Ruiz, in her excellent history of Mexican American women *From Out of the Shadows*, describes Chicanas involved in the Chicano movement as identifying either as "feminists" or as "loyalists". The feminists worked hard to have women's issues heard and included in the movement's platforms and were often forced out for their trouble. The loyalists thought it more important to postpone their feminist concerns until the struggle for Aztlán and equal rights for *la raza* was successful. Some Chicanas viewed the precedent of the "Adelitas" or *soldaderas* as a helpful compromise, those women who fought alongside their men during the Mexican revolution—independent women who also took care of the "macho."

When Chicanas organized, they worked to improve the community as a whole, improving their sisters' lives and situations. "As farm hands, cannery workers, miners' wives, *mutualista*[2] members, club women, civil rights advocates, and politicians, Mexican women have taken direct action for themselves and others" (Ruiz 73). As labor leaders, Chicanas were tireless and fearless. In San Antonio, they played a major role in the Pecan Shellers' strike of 1938. When their wages were cut by a penny a pound, the shellers walked out in protest and many were beaten and arrested. Former Housing and Urban Development secretary Henry Cisneros's mother-in-law was one of those workers. Another, *La Pasionaria*, passionate and fiery Emma Tenayuca was instrumental in organizing the successful 37-day strike. After agreeing to arbitration under the new National Labor Relations Act, the plant operators raised wages to 25 cents an hour.

In Silver City, New Mexico, the iconic "Salt of the Earth" strike was saved by Chicanas: Mexican miners walked off their jobs over wage and safety issues in October 1950. When the miners were threatened with jail, their wives took their places on the picket line while the men took care of domestic duties and the children. Even though they were assaulted and arrested, the women refused to be intimidated. Three of the wives who held the line became members of the team negotiating for the union. Their ability to reach an arbitrated settlement in favor of the families became one of the few labor victories achieved during the 1950s. "The movie *Salt of the Earth* remains emblematic of a long history of labor activism among Mexican women in the United States" (Ruiz 85–86).

In the area of social services, Chicanas spearheaded life-changing projects in their neighborhoods and barrios. They provided safe places where welfare mothers and working women could meet and discuss their challenges and disappointments, frustrations and successes, and their children and their own lives. The Chicana Welfare Rights Organization in Los Angeles began this way. This is where women discovered the fact that they had been sterilized without their consent. Chicana lawyers who were fresh out of law school worked with the *Comisión Femenil Mexicana* and filed suit on behalf of 12 of these women. Although they lost the case, they were successful at bringing attention and censure to the shameful practice of coercing sterilization on poor women of color, prompting hospitals to change their policies and practice.

Chicanas had been advocating for equal rights since entering the labor force. They identified with the women's movement but felt it was overly focused on individual liberty and personal advancement while it belittled their cultural and working-class concerns. Women like Rosie Castro and Elizabeth "Betita" Martínez strove to raise their whole community up; their leadership paradigm sought to empower others. In a scorching critique of the Eurocentric, middle-class orientation of the women's movement, authors and activists Cherríe Moraga and Gloria Anzaldúa put together an anthology by women of color—including lesbians who brought forth their particular concerns for respect and recognition—and plotted their own path toward liberation. In order to bring *This Bridge Called My Back* to fruition, Moraga and Anzaldúa created their own publishing house—Kitchen Table Women of Color Press—and published the book in 1981.

Chicanas have been prolific writers since the beginning of the Chicano movement, publishing many of the newspapers as well as poetry and prose. "Betita" Martínez, who published *500 Years of Chicana Women's History* in 2008, founded *El Grito del Norte* in 1968 in Española, New Mexico. In 1971, Ana Nieto Gómez founded *Hijas de Cuauhtémoc* at California State University at Long Beach, which evolved into *Encuentro Femenil*, the first scholarly Chicana journal. When she was elected president of MEChA (Movimiento Estudiantil Chicano De Aztlán), the male students hung her in effigy, an example of how contentious gender relations were at that time and how virulent male opposition to women's liberation was. In Los Angeles in 1970, Francisca Flores published and edited *Regeneración* in the spirit of the magazine of the same name published by the anarchist Flores Magón brothers during the Mexican revolution. Francisca Flores was an activist since the early days; she had worked on the Sleepy Lagoon defense in the 1940s,[3] helped organize clandestine showings of *The Salt of the Earth* film in the 1950s; she was a cofounder of the Mexican American Political Association (MAPA), the *Comisión Femenil Mexicana* and the Chicana Social Service Center, serving as its first director. In San Bernardino, California, Gloria Macías Harrison established *El Chicano* and continues to write a column for this weekly. Through their writings, Chicanas problematized and challenged prescribed gender roles at home (familial oligarchy), at school (the home economics track), and at meetings (the cleanup committee) (Ruiz 107–8).

Whether feminist, loyalist, or Adelita, Chicanas made significant contributions to the Chicano movement. From the young Chicana Brown Berets to students like Vicky Castro and Paula Crisóstomo, key organizers of the Walk Outs, to Dolores Huerta with the United Farm Workers' Association, to Rosie Castro with La Raza Unida Party, all of the Chicano movement organizations counted on female support, strength, and passion for justice. In a statement that could have spoken for most Chicanas involved in the movement, Texas Chicanas/Tejanas made clear to their male counterparts when they barged into La Raza Unida Party organizational meetings to declare, "we don't want to be the tamale makers and . . . the busy bees. We really want to be part of the decision-making process" (Ruiz 116).

## ABOUT SANDRA CISNEROS, "HER POWER IS HER OWN"

What a storied life Sandra Cisneros has led! From the barrios of Chicago to Iowa's Writers' Workshop to San Antonio to Guanajuato, Mexico, with time spent in Massachusetts, California, and Europe, Cisneros has lived her life by her passions, and lucky for us, her overriding passion is writing. When she puts pen to paper, she crafts poetry and prose that is delicious, wicked, intense, eye-opening, and change-bringing; her work has spoken to millions of readers since she published her first piece in Josephinum Catholic High School's literary journal before she graduated in 1972.

Her fairy tale started as the only girl in a family of seven children like the little sister in the Grimm's tale *Six Swans* who rescues her six brothers who have been transformed into swans: "In Spanish our name means swan. /A great past—castles maybe / or a Sahara city, / but more likely / a name that stuck / to a barefoot boy / herding the dusty flock / down the bright road ["Six Brothers," *My Wicked Wicked Ways* 25). Besides being the only, lonely girl while her brothers all paired off, Cisneros was brought up in a Mexican American working-class family. The family dynamic was similar to what many of us who grew up in the 1950s and 1960s experienced: an emotionally distant, working father and a frustrated stay-at-home mother. In Cisneros's case, her father was a first-generation Mexican immigrant who was proud of coming from a "good" family and regularly uprooted the family to travel to Mexico City to visit his mother, a ritual Cisneros brings to life in her novel *Caramelo*. After a stint in World War II where he earned U.S. citizenship instead of deportation, her Papa Fernando Cisneros got to Chicago, fell in love with and married Elvira Cordero Anguiano, and went to work in her family's upholstery business. Elvira was the favorite daughter who, while she also fell in love, married

Fernando in part to escape her own desperate family situation but ended up disappointed with her lot in life. She resented having her dreams deferred but made up for it by taking the family to the library every Saturday and to museums on Sundays. In the vignette "A Smart Cookie," Esperanza's mother laments, "I could've been somebody, you know?" (91), a sentiment that voiced many of our mothers' regrets.

By the fifth grade, Sandra Cisneros had decided that she would go to college. Her father supported that ambition, thinking it would be the best place for her to find a good husband. Cisneros had other ideas and while the daughter who "burned the rice" helped at home where she could—she was "too daydreamy to learn how to cook" (*House of My Own* 295), her mother gave her space and time to read, study, and write, while keeping her brothers at bay. Cisneros won a scholarship to Loyola University in Chicago and, after attending a creative writing workshop there, found the path she would follow with such devotion, later making the decision never to marry or have children. "Nobody's wife and nobody's mother,"[4] she has dedicated her life to her work and to her community. After being accepted to the prestigious Iowa Writers' Workshop program, her experience in the Master of Fine Arts program was dominated by culture shock for Cisneros. Once again, she felt the odd woman out. Her life experience was very different from the other students, who were mostly from white, upper- or middle-class backgrounds.

After graduation, Cisneros went to work at an alternative high school as it did not occur to her to seek academic employment at a college or university. Through it all, she continued to write and refine her work. She began working on *The House on Mango Street* in Iowa and continued to weave the stories and fashion the characters and their situations from people she met—from the barrio, from her students, from the high school dropouts she worked with at the alternative school, and from her travels. She structured *Mango Street* as a book that could be read easily; any person could pick it up and take up the story at any point. Like a string of pearls, each vignette could be appreciated on its own or form a coherent story when read all the way through.

Author Gary Soto had encountered her poetry on a visit to Chicago and encouraged Sandra to submit stories for "chapbooks," pamphlet-like books Chicanos were producing in California. Her chapbook *Bad Boys* impressed Dr. Nicolás Kanellos who offered Sandra her first contract to publish her novel through his Arte Público Press. With that advance and the money from a National Endowment for the Arts (NEA) grant, she was able to travel to Europe. While in Europe, she spent time as an artist in residence at an artists' foundation in Venice, Italy. During her travels, she found that she was most likely to find support, guidance, and *comadrazgo*, a feeling of companionship and solidarity, among women wherever she happened to be.

After the success of *Mango Street* and her books of poetry and short stories, Cisneros won important recognitions including another NEA grant and a MacArthur genius grant (then founding the Latino MacArturitos dedicated to community outreach). Her books have won numerous awards and accolades. *The House on Mango Street* is read and discussed in classrooms from middle schools to universities. Sandra Cisneros has transcended the somewhat narrow focus sometimes suffered by "ethnic" authors; her work has attained best-seller status, and new books are eagerly anticipated by readers around the world and have been translated into over a dozen languages. She has used her influence judiciously to nurture writers through her own foundations—the Macondo Foundation and the Alfredo Cisneros del Moral Foundation—and is unfailingly thoughtful, fearless, and kind in her public speaking and writing.

## WHY WE READ *THE HOUSE ON MANGO STREET*

Sandra Cisneros, keeper of swans, writes poetry, and writes prose that is like music, like flowers, like a rock through a window, like a slap in the face! To create *The House on Mango Street,* she took a stone *molcajete*, threw in a handful of burned rice; the bruises, tears, and laughter of friends and neighbors; the clouds and laments of high school dropouts; and a pinch of *Dream Tigers* and fairy tales mixed in with the fear, loneliness, and alienation of a young artist *hija de papi* surrounded by spoiled gringo brats. She took this *mejurje*, kneaded it, worked it, beat it, and whipped it up with the strength of her convictions, her innate sense of justice, her passion, and the exhilaration of words put together in just the right way. The icing on this *Mango pastel* is beautiful simplicity—simple words, and simple stories about everyday people.

Sandra Cisneros's dedication to her craft continues to resonate with a wide range of readers, and she has gained the respect of the literary community around the world. She is an author who creates works with heart, the heart that has guided her life choices privately and as a public figure. Her words and her work speak to millions of readers and women who recognize themselves in her stories and her poetry. *The House on Mango*

*Street* speaks *A las mujeres*/To the women and validates Chicana's life experiences, giving them a space to dream and to hope.

*The House on Mango Street* is a girl's coming-of-age story. The feminine version of the bildungsroman traditionally ended with the girl accepting her subordinate role in a patriarchal society as she enters adulthood as a young woman. Sandra Cisneros turned that tradition on its head with her story of a girl unsatisfied with her assigned role who decides to construct her own place in the world and forge the way for the other women in her community. Through the depictions in *The House on Mango Street*, Chicana women's experience of subordination, oppression, violence (domestic and otherwise), marginalization, and objectification are externalized and validated; damaging archetypes are acknowledged and transformed into empowering ones.

One archetype that Chicana and Mexican women have struggled with since the Spanish Conquista is the legacy of Malinalli aka La Malinche aka Doña Marina aka Malintzin, Conquistador Hernan Cortés' interpreter despised as Mexico's original traitor. Chicana literary critic Norma Alarcon's essay in *This Bridge Called My Back* explores how the Malinche myth haunts Chicana authors: "it seeps into our own consciousness in the cradle . . . we may come to believe that indeed our very sexuality condemns us to enslavement. An enslavement which is subsequently manifested as self-hatred. All we see is hatred of women" (*This Bridge* 183).

Esperanza in *The House on Mango Street* witnesses this enslavement, hatred, and self-hatred and transcends it to come out stronger. The examples of female powerlessness and self-hatred start in her own home, from her captive, wild grandmother to her frustrated mother. In the barrio, she encounters many Rapunzel-like figures: Mamacita who doesn't speak English and cries all day from homesickness and loneliness; Marin waiting for a handsome prince to notice her and carry her away; Rafaela who gets the kids to send her papaya juice up in a paper bag on a string; Rosa Vargas, abandoned by her husband, who has so many children she can't keep track of them; Alicia afraid of mice who goes to college but has to heed her father telling her "a woman's place is sleeping so she can wake up early with the tortilla star" (31); Minerva who writes poems but "comes over black and blue" (85); and poor, dangerously beautiful Sally beaten and abused by her father and later, the husband she hoped would be her knight in shining armor—the marshmallow salesman.

The character from the episode "Edna's Ruthie" is living the exact opposite of the life Esperanza wants for her future self. She embodies the fate that awaits Esperanza if her escape from Mango Street is not successful.

Ruthie is popular with the children because, like a poet, "she sees lovely things everywhere" (68) and makes lyrical observations like "The moon is beautiful like a balloon" and tells Esperanza that she "used to write children's books once" (69). Esperanza declares that Ruthie had all kinds of job offers and "There were many things Ruthie could have been if she wanted to" (68) but instead got married and now she is a virtual prisoner at her mother's apartment house on Mango Street. Hers is the future we can see for Esperanza if she doesn't take steps that will empower rather than imprison her—devoured like the oysters in the "Walrus and the Carpenter" poem that she recites for Ruthie, bringing tears to her eyes with the observation that Esperanza "has the most beautiful teeth [she's] ever seen" (69), suitable for munching on oysters we assume.

Although Esperanza rejects Mango Street, by the end of the book she has acknowledged that she also *is* Mango Street "Like it or not" as her friend Alicia (the one afraid of mice) tells her. They laugh at the idea of the mayor coming out to improve Mango Street as Esperanza requires for her return. The tacit understanding is that she will indeed return to "make it better" since somebody has to. Like La Malinche, she will leave her barrio, but unlike her, Esperanza will return to build up, not to abandon or betray.

Before *The House on Mango Street* was published, mainstream novels by Chicanas were few and far between. Chicana authors who have had some success include Denise Chavez, Ana Castillo (who translated *This Bridge Called My Back* into Spanish), and Lucha Corpi. From Las Cruces, New Mexico, Chavez has published *The Last of the Menu Girls* (1986), *The Face of an Angel* (1994), and *Loving Pedro Infante* (2001) as well as poetry and plays. Her latest novel is *The King and Queen of Comezon* (2014). Ana Castillo, like Sandra Cisneros, is from Chicago. Her novels include *The Mixquiahala Letters* (1986), an epistolary novel in the style of Julio Cortázar's *Hopscotch*, *Peel My Love Like an Onion* (1999) and *The Guardians* (2007). She continues to push boundaries, both literary and sexual, in her latest work *Give It to Me* (2014). Born in Mexico and transplanted to California, Lucha Corpi wrote a series of detective novels featuring Chicana private investigator Gloria Damasco. The point of departure for the first novel *Eulogy for a Brown Angel* (1992) is a boy's murder committed during the Chicano Moratorium in Los Angeles in 1970.

Non-Chicana Latina authors who have contributed literature from a female immigrant perspective include Dominican Julia Alvarez with her novel *How the Garcia Girls Lost Their Accent* (1991), her most recent novel is *Saving the World* (2006); and Cuban American Cristina García, author of *Dreaming in Cuban* (1992), *The Agüero Sisters* (1997), *Lady*

*Matador's Hotel* (2010), and, her latest, *King of Cuba* (2013). Like Sandra Cisneros, out of the hard life of Latinas in the United States, these authors have made art.

Cisneros set out to make art that would make a difference in the world. Her book brought Chicanas' stories and situations into the public view. As she later expressed in a heartfelt letter to a woman who asked to have *The House on Mango Street* removed from her child's school library— "I strongly believe the work of community outreach is part of my task of healing and making nonviolent social change in a time of extreme fear and xenophobia" (*House of My Own* 309). Just as Esperanza resolved to return for "those who cannot out," Sandra Cisneros continues to dedicate her work and her life to the highest standards.

## HISTORICAL EXPLORATIONS

Since the Spanish Conquista sank its roots in to this continent, Mexican women have been cursed with the legacy of La Malinche, Doña Marina. La Malinche, the much-maligned woman considered the *gran chingada* betrayer of her people, is the archetype represented by Marin in *The House on Mango Street*. *Chingada* is one of the most often used curse words in Mexico and the United States among Chicanos; it literally means to be raped or fucked. Malintzin was born into Aztec royalty and sold into slavery. By all accounts, she was a quick study, especially at languages. Her skilled interpreting brought her to translate for Captain Hernan Cortés, engineer of the conquest, and she soon became indispensable. He took her as a mistress and fathered a son by her (Martín Cortés, the first *mestizo*).

Between a woman and a man, attitudes toward this story would bring very different interpretations, and because mostly men have written history, Doña Marina has become the symbol for anyone who turns his/her back on their *patria*, Mexico. People who are perceived to value foreign ways over Mexican ones are denigratingly called *Malinchistas*. For Mexican and Chicana women, Malinche's legacy has been devastating, leaving them, according to men at least, doomed to promiscuity and pain.

Another fierce woman venerated in Mexican History—her image adorns the 200 peso note—is Sor Juana Ines de la Cruz. Sor Juana was an extremely intelligent, creative woman with an inquiring mind. Like Sandra Cisneros so many centuries later, she decided against having a husband and family in order to pursue her passion—her studies and her writing. Thus she entered the convent, but even there, she was challenged and punished for her radical views and for speaking her mind.

Esperanza herself is, of course, most like Sor Juana as she declares, "I have decided not to grow up tame like the others who lay their necks on the threshold waiting for the ball and chain" (88). Like Sor Juana, she revels in her ability to create, to be original. Her quick mind shows up in the "And Some More" vignette, for example, where Esperanza, as she plays with words, comes up with sounds and names, ever expanding the game, beginning with clouds:

> There are all different kinds of clouds. How many different kinds of clouds can you think of?
> Well, there's these already that look like shaving cream . . .
> And what about the kind that looks like you combed its hair? . . .
> And don't forget nimbus the rain cloud . . .
> There's that wide puffy cloud that looks like your face when you wake up after falling asleep with all your clothes on . . .
> I can think of thirty Eskimo words for you, Rachel. Thirty words that say what you are.
> . . .
> . . . you're like foot fleas, that's you.
> Chicken lips.
> Cockroach jelly.
> Cold *frijoles*. (36–37)

Later in the "Hips" episode, she again riffs on the traditional jump-roping rhymes with her friends and gets frustrated with her sister Nenny who insists on repeating the same old songs with no frills or variations. "Not that old song, I say. You gotta use your own song. Make it up, you know?" (52)

Esperanza rejects the role models she finds on Mango Street and instead finds inspiration in "Four Skinny Trees":

> Four skinny trees with skinny necks and pointy elbows like mine. Four who do not belong here but are here. . . . Their strength is secret. . . . They grow up and they grow down and grab the earth between their hairy toes and bite the sky with violent teeth and never quit their anger. . . . When I am too sad and too skinny to keep keeping, when I am a tiny thing against so many bricks, then it is I look at trees. (74–75)

The tree's fierce spirit is one that Mexican and Chicana women have employed since the times of Doña Marina. Josefa Ortiz de Domínguez, la Corregidora, is a fierce woman from Mexican history who played a key role in Mexican independence. La Corregidora, although she was the wife of a colonial bureaucrat, conspired and helped the rebels organize effective military strategies against the Spanish royalists.

In the 20th century, invoking the fierce spirit of the *soldaderas*—women who fought alongside the men in the Mexican revolution—Chicanas have been effective activists in labor movements: from Emma Tenayuca in Texas to the women in New Mexico mines featured in the movie *The Salt of the Earth*, to the women striking for equality in Watsonville canneries, to the great Dolores Huerta, one of Cesar Chavez's most valued organizers for the United Farm Workers.

The women's movement in the U.S. grew out of women's frustration with their relegated, subordinate roles and treatment in the student organizations that participated in the Civil Rights Movement of the 1960s. After reading books like Betty Friedan's *The Feminine Mystique* (1963), middle-class women woke up to the fact that they had been oppressed, their potential stifled, and they are imprisoned in the suburbs. The women's movement brought attention to the unequal treatment of women throughout society, raising consciousness about everything from reproductive rights to the sexual objectification of women to the lack of female political representation to wage disparity. Since Chicanas had been advocating for equal rights since they entered the labor force, the women's movement presented a welcome opportunity for solidarity. Chicanas participated in the International Women's conference in Mexico City, and in 1977, the National Women's Conference in Houston brought together Chicanas and feminists from all over the country. A few years later, Sandra Cisneros was working on *The House on Mango Street*, and Moraga and Anzaldúa were working on their seminal book *This Bridge Called My Back*.

In the early 1970s, Chicanas began to advocate for their issues to be addressed in Mexican American and Chicano groups. They created a caucus within the California group MAPA, a group established in 1959 dedicated to building the political power of Mexican Americans. They created a women's caucus in the La Raza Unida Party called Mujeres por La Raza. They held forums on women's issues at universities like California State University at Los Angeles. The Mexican American National Issues Forum that was held in Sacramento in 1970 included a workshop on women.

In May 1971, Chicanas mobilized nationwide and organized a conference that took place in Houston with 600 delegates from 23 states. Although the divisions among loyalists and feminists prompted 40 percent of the delegates to leave, charging racism on the part of the YWCA—the organization sponsoring the conference—the plan they produced at that conference contained resolutions outlining their support for women's issues within the context of the Chicano movement.

An homage to Sandra Cisneros's Chicano heritage, *The House on Mango Street* dances with affection and solidarity for the people and culture in the barrio through the novel's warm depictions of family and daily life. Chicano male characters are hardworking fathers and supportive uncles, and, in one case, a lonely undocumented working man live next door to the "macho"[5] abusers and wife beaters. Cisneros's is a multilayered, truthful portrayal of the Chicano's marginalized situation that duplicates and compounds the marginalization of Chicanas.

For Esperanza, the hard reality of discrimination and shaming shared by most poor women of color begins with the nuns' attitudes. Their disdain marginalizes her but also gives her a sense of solidarity with her barrio:

> You live *there?*
>      *There.* I had to look to where she pointed-the third floor, the paint peeling, wooden bars Papa had nailed on the windows so we wouldn't fall out. . . . You live *there?* The way she said it made me feel like nothing. *There.* I lived *there.* I nodded. (5)

And later during the "Rice Sandwich" episode: "Which one is your house? . . . That one? She pointed to a row of ugly three-flats, the ones even the raggedy men are ashamed to go into" (45)

From these feelings of shame, Esperanza becomes determined to lift her community as expressed in the "Bums in the Attic" episode. She declares that she wants a house not only to rise above the embarrassment felt with the nuns but also to share with those less fortunate. She becomes aware of class differences on the weekend drives the family takes to admire the houses on the hill "like the ones with the gardens where Papa works." She later refuses to accompany the family on these excursions because "People who live on hills sleep so close to the stars they forget those of us who live too much on earth. They don't look down at all except to be content to live on hills. The have nothing to do with last week's garbage or fear of rats." Esperanza has flipped her shame into an inclusive idealistic plan for her own house on the hill—"I won't forget who I am or where I came from. Passing bums will ask, Can I come in? I'll offer them the attic, ask them to stay, because I know how it is to be without a house" (86–87).

Esperanza's father is a hardworking man who loves his family. She expresses her appreciation for his sacrifices in the episode where he tells Esperanza about her grandfather's death, "Your *abuelito* is dead . . . and then as if he just heard the news himself, crumples like a coat and cries, my brave Papa cries. . . . My Papa, has thick hands and thick shoes, who wakes up tired in the dark, who combs his hair with water, drinks his coffee, and is gone before we wake (56–57).

Her uncle is another man who lifts Esperanza up. In the heartwarming "Chanclas" episode, Esperanza is obliged to wear her old school shoes to her cousin's baptism party because her exhausted mother forgot to buy new shoes to go with her new party dress:

> Then Uncle Nacho is pulling and pulling my arm and it doesn't matter how new the dress Mama bought is because my feet are ugly until my uncle who is a liar says, You are the prettiest girl here, will you dance, but I believe him, and yes, we are dancing, my Uncle Nacho and me, only I don't want to at first. My feet swell big and heavy like plungers, but I drag them across the linoleum floor straight center where Uncle wants to show off the new dance we learned. And Uncle spins me, and my skinny arms bend the way he taught me . . . and everyone says, wow, who are those two who dance like in the movies, until I forget that I am wearing only ordinary shoes, brown and white, the kind my mother buys each year for school. (47)

Although "Geraldo No Last Name" does not belong to Esperanza's immediate family, his vignette provides a poignant acknowledgement of undocumented workers as part of the Chicano family. Marin met Geraldo at a dance. Afterward, he is hit by a car and she must explain:

> Once to the hospital people and twice to the police. No address. No name. Nothing in his pockets. Ain't it a shame.
> . . . Nobody but an intern working all alone. And maybe if the surgeon would've come, maybe if he hadn't lost so much blood, if the surgeon had only come, they would know who to notify and where. . . . He wasn't anything to her. . . . Just another *brazer* who didn't speak English. Just another wetback. You know the kind. The ones who always look ashamed. . . . Geraldo in his shiny shirt and green pants. . . . They never saw the kitchenettes. They never knew about the two-room flats and sleeping rooms he rented, the weekly money orders sent home, the currency exchange. How could they?
> His name was Geraldo. And his home in another country. The ones he left behind are far away, will wonder, shrug, remember. Geraldo—he went north . . . we never heard from him again. (66)

Esperanza's neighbor Louie's episode features a glimpse of crime in the barrio and its proximity to the marginalized families on Mango Street. Louie's cousin gives the kids a ride in his new yellow Cadillac right before the police catch up with him:

> "The seats were big and soft like a sofa. . ." when they hear police sirens, "Louie's cousin stopped the car right where we were and said, Everybody out of the car . . . we ran down the block to where the cop car's siren spun

a dizzy blue. The nose of that yellow Cadillac was all pleated like an alligator's, and except a bloody lip and a bruised forehead, Louie's cousin was okay. They put handcuffs on him and put him in the backseat of the cop car, and we all waved as they drove away." (24–25)

In stark contrast to its positive male characters, *The House on Mango Street* is populated by many more "macho" men, those who are violent and abusive toward their wives and daughters and then regretful (Sally's father); the men who seek out infantile, "nonthreatening" women as mates (Sire); and the anonymous men who harass and rape.

"What Sally Said" is a painful vignette to read; a spot-on portrayal of a child victim's experience—the physical pain, the collusive mother, the victim making excuses for her tormentor:

He never hits me hard. She said her mama rubs lard on all the places where it hurts. Then at school she'd say she fell. That's where all the blue places come from. That's why her skin is always scarred. . . .

But Sally doesn't tell about that time he hit her with his hands just like a dog, she said, like if I was an animal . . .

Sally was going to get permission to stay with us a little . . . except when the dark came her father, whose eyes were little from crying, knocked on the door and said please come back, this is the last time . . .

Until one day Sally's father catches her talking to a boy. . . . Until the way Sally tells, it, he just went crazy, he just forgot he was her father between the buckle and the belt.

You're not my daughter, you're not my daughter. And then he broke into his hands. [93]

"Sire" is the man—punk according to her father—who looks at Esperanza (who fearlessly looks right back at him) but has chosen a girlfriend who can't even tie her own shoes, "She is tiny and pretty and smells like baby's skin. . . . I saw her barefoot baby toenails all painted pale pale pink, like little pink seashells, and she smells pink like babies do. . . . But she doesn't know how to tie her shoes. I do" (73).

The anonymous and not so anonymous harassers and tormentors populate much of the novel. For example, in "The Family of Little Feet" episode, Esperanza and her pals try out their sex appeal with that family's discarded high heels. "Today we are Cinderella . . . [and tee-totter] down to the corner where the men can't take their eyes off us" (40); one man tells them that the shoes are dangerous and that he will call the police on them; a boy calls out "Ladies, lead me to heaven" (41); finally a bum offers Rachel $1 for a kiss and they run "fast and far away" and nobody complains when the shoes get thrown away.

Esperanza herself confronts disturbing instances of sexual assault and possibly rape. At her first job, she is manhandled by a man she had looked on as a supportive friend. In "The Red Clowns" episode, she feels betrayed by Sally: "Why didn't you hear me when I called? Why didn't you tell them to leave me alone? The one who grabbed me by the arm, he wouldn't let me go" (100). These episodes and the way Sandra Cisneros portrays them as devastating and deeply wounding constituted valuable contributions to the dialogue about rape and sexual harassment. Attitudes toward rape have changed drastically in the last few decades. It was not so long ago that rape and sexual abuse were not viewed as serious offenses and the victim was often blamed and shamed.

Single women with dependent children are another vulnerable group that Chicanas championed, for example, in their opposition to the proposed Talmadge Amendment of 1973. The proposal was to require women on public assistance (welfare) with children over six years old to register with the state employment office every two weeks until they found a job, with no provisions made for child care! Recent "welfare to work" legislation harkens back to this type of shortsighted proposal and is born of a similar prejudice. For Rosa Vargas, the "Old Woman She Had So Many Children She Didn't Know What to Do" who cannot keep up with all her kids—"It's not her fault you know, except she is their mother and only one against so many" (29) and the neighborhood also gives up trying to control or keep track of them: "nobody looked up not once the day Angel Vargas learned to fly and dropped from the sky like a sugar donut, just like a falling star, and exploded down to earth without even an "Oh" (30)—such a requirement would have been impossible to meet and in effect, Cisneros vividly presents the lethal consequences of inadequate support for mothers with dependent children.

*The House on Mango Street* brought to life and put in context the issues that Chicanas worked so hard to bring to the awareness of their male counterparts—violence against women, support for mothers with small children, sexual harassment, and, underlying all, gender equality.

# DOCUMENTING *THE HOUSE ON MANGO STREET*

## Fierce Women in Chicano History

Sandra Cisneros is of the opinion that throughout Mexican and Chicano history, women were fierce in spite of their reputation for being docile and submissive. The first document presents the archetypal figure of Malinche from a human perspective. The second document is Sor Juan Ines de la Cruz's poem about men's silly and contradictory, hypocritical and unrealistic expectations when it comes to women. Author Gloria Anzaldúa returns to the theme of Malinche in the third document, celebrating her indigenous heritage in the struggle on behalf of all indigenous women.

## From *Introduction to Malintzin Tenépal: A Preliminary Look into a New Perspective*, 1977

History, literature and popular belief normally introduce us to the story and image of Doña Marina, La Malinche, in either of three ways: (1) the woman is oftentimes presented very simply and insignificantly as just another part of the necessary back-drop to Cortés' triumphant conquest or, as is more commonly done, (2) her portrayal assumes synonymity with destruction when she is singled out as the sole cause of the fall of the "patria" and becomes the scapegoat for all Mexican perdition thereafter while, on the other hand, (3) romanticists find themselves almost instinctively driven to depicting Doña Marina as the misguided and exploited victim of the tragic love affair which is said to have taken place between herself and Hernán Cortés.

The above approaches for depiction of Doña Marina do no justice to the image of this Mexican woman in that the following historical aspects are not taken into full consideration:

1. Quetzalcoatl—the prophet and his religion;
2. Aztec religion—in particular, the works of Tlacaelel;
3. The political milieu of the Aztec empire at the time of the conquest;
4. The situation of the Indian peoples under Aztec rule;
5. Marina's personal life;
6. Her actual deeds in the conquest of México, and finally,
7. Speculation based on all of the above concerning Doña Marina's motives for having involved herself in the conquest.

Only after all of the above historical aspects have been carefully considered can a comprehensive account of Doña Marina's behavior be given, for her actions were contingent upon the historical events of her time.

Doña Marina is significant in that she embodies effective, decisive action in the feminine form, and most important, because her own actions syncretized two conflicting worlds causing the emergence of a new one—our own. Here, woman acts not as a goddess in some mythology, but as an actual force in the making of history.

*Source:* Adelaida R. del Castillo, *Essays on la mujer* (Los Angeles, CA: Chicano Studies Center Publications, 1977), 124–125.

# From *Hombres Necios Que Acusáis/ A La Mujer Sin Razón*, 1680

Hombres necios que acusáis
a la mujer sin razón,
sin ver que sois la ocasión
de lo mismo que culpáis:

si con ansia sin igual
solicitáis su desdén,
¿por qué quereis que obren bien
si las incitáis al mal?

Combatís su resistencia
y luego, con gravedad,
decís que fue liviandad
lo que hizo la diligencia.

Parecer quiere el denuedo
de vuestro parecer loco,
al niño que pone el coco
y luego le tiene miedo.

Queréis, con presunción necia,
hallar a la que buscáis,
para pretendida, Thais,
y en la posesión, Lucrecia

¿Qué humor puede ser más raro
que el que, falto de consejo,
el mismo empaña el espejo
y siente que no esté claro?

Con el favor y el desdén
tenéis condición igual,
quejándoos, si os tratan mal,
burlándoos, si os quieren bien.

Opinión, ninguna gana:
pues la que más se recata,
si no os admite, es ingrata,
y si os admite, es liviana

Siempre tan necios andáis
que, con desigual nivel,
a una culpáis por crüel
y a otra por fácil culpáis.

¿Pues cómo ha de estar templada
la que vuestro amor pretende,
si la que es ingrata, ofende,
y la que es fácil, enfada?

Mas, entre el enfado y pena
que vuestro gusto refiere,
bien haya la que no os quiere
y quejaos en hora buena.

Dan vuestras amantes penas
a sus libertades alas,
y después de hacerlas malas
las queréis hallar muy buenas.

¿Cuál mayor culpa ha tenido
en una pasión errada:
la que cae de rogada
o el que ruega de caído?

¿O cuál es más de culpar,
aunque cualquiera mal haga:
la que peca por la paga
o el que paga por pecar?

Pues ¿para qué os espantáis
de la culpa que tenéis?
Queredlas cual las hacéis
o hacedlas cual las buscáis.

Dejad de solicitar,
y después, con más razón,
acusaréis la afición
de la que os fuere a rogar.

Bien con muchas armas fundo
que lidia vuestra arrogancia,
pues en promesa e instancia
juntáis diablo, carne y mundo.

(English) In a Lighter Vein
Silly, you men-so very adept
at wrongly faulting womankind,

not seeing you're alone to blame
for faults you plant in woman's mind.

After you've won by urgent plea
the right to tarnish her good name,
you still expect her to behave—
you, that coaxed her into shame.

You batter her resistance down
and then, all righteousness, proclaim
that feminine frivolity,
not your persistence, is to blame.

When it comes to bravely posturing,
your witlessness must take the prize:
you're the child that makes a bogeyman,
and then recoils in fear and cries.

Presumptuous beyond belief,
you'd have the woman you pursue
be Thais when you're courting her,
Lucretia once she falls to you.

For plain default of common sense,
could any action be so queer
as oneself to cloud the mirror,
then complain that it's not clear?

Whether you're favored or disdained,
nothing can leave you satisfied.
You whimper if you're turned away,
you sneer if you've been gratified.

With you, no woman can hope to score;
whichever way, she's bound to lose;
spurning you, she's ungrateful—
succumbing, you call her lewd.

Your folly is always the same:
you apply a single rule
to the one you accuse of looseness
and the one you brand as cruel.

What happy mean could there be
for the woman who catches your eye,
if, unresponsive, she offends,
yet whose complaisance you decry?

Still, whether it's torment or anger—
and both ways you've yourselves to blame—
God bless the woman who won't have you,
no matter how loud you complain.

It's your persistent entreaties
that change her from timid to bold.
Having made her thereby naughty,
you would have her good as gold.

So where does the greater guilt lie
for a passion that should not be:
with the man who pleads out of baseness
or the woman debased by his plea?

Or which is more to be blamed—
though both will have cause for chagrin:
the woman who sins for money
or the man who pays money to sin?

So why are you men all so stunned
at the thought you're all guilty alike?
Either like them for what you've made them
or make of them what you can like.

If you'd give up pursuing them,
you'd discover, without a doubt,
you've a stronger case to make
against those who seek you out.

I well know what powerful arms
you wield in pressing for evil:
your arrogance is allied
with the world, the flesh, and the devil!

*Source: A Sor Juana Anthology*, translated by Alan S. Trueblood, Foreword by Octavio Paz, Cambridge, MA: Harvard University Press, Copyright © 1988 by the President and Fellows of Harvard College.

# From *The Wounding of the India-Mestiza*, 1987

*Estas carnes indias que despreciamos nosotros los mexicanos asi como despreciamos condenamos a Nuestra madre, Malinali. Nos condenamos a nuestros mismos. Esta raza vencida, enemigo cuerpo.*

Not me sold out my people but they me. *Malinal Tenepat*, or *Malintzin*, has become known as *la Chingada*—the fucked one. She has become the bad word that passes a dozen times a day from the lips of Chicanos. Whore, prostitute, the woman who sold out her people to the Spaniards are epithets Chicanos spit out with contempt.

The worst kind of betrayal lies in making us believe that the Indian woman in us is the betrayer. We, *indias y mestizas*, police the Indian in us, brutalize and condemn her. Male culture has done a good job on us. *Son las costumbres que traicionan. La india en mí en la sombra: La Chingada, Tlazolteotl, Coatlicue. Sonellas que oyemos lamentando a sus hijas perdidas.*

Not me sold out my people but they me. Because of the color of my skin they betrayed me. The dark-skinned woman has been silenced, gagged, caged, bound into servitude with marriage, bludgeoned for 300 years she has been a slave, a force of cheap labor, colonized by the Spaniard, the Anglo, by her own people (and in Mesoamerica her lot under the Indian patriarchs was not free of wounding). For 300 years she was invisible, she was not heard. Many times she wished to speak, to act, to protest, to challenge. The odds were heavily against her. She hid her feelings; she hid her truths; she concealed her fire; but she kept stoking the inner flame. She remained faceless and voiceless, but a light shone through her veil of silence. And though she was unable to spread her limbs and though for her right now the sun has sunk under the earth and there is no moon, she continues to tend the flame. The spirit of the fire spurs her to fight for her own skin and a piece of ground to stand on, a ground from which to view the world—a perspective, a home ground where she can plumb the rich ancestral roots into her own ample *mestiza* heart. She waits till the waters are not so turbulent and the mountains not so slippery with sleet. Battered and bruised she waits, her bruises throwing her back upon herself and the rhythmic pulse of the feminine *Coatlalopeuh* waits with her.

*Aquí en la soledad prospera su rebeldía.*

*En la soledad Ella prospera.*

Source: Gloria Anzaldúa, *Borderlands/La Frontera: The New Mestiza* (San Francisco, CA: Aunt Lute Books, 1987), 44–45. Reprinted with permission.

## Chicanisma and the First Chicana National Conference

The documents in this section portray the unique challenge Chicanas faced as the Chicano movement progressed. They were expected to support Aztlán and Chicano nationalism while postponing their own liberation; on the other hand, the larger feminist movement did not make the race and class discrimination faced by Chicanas a priority. In the first document, the writer laments the fact that at a Raza conference she attended, the "consensus" was that Chicana women did not want to be liberated and proceeds to explain why they do, recalling the Chicana heritage of "fierce" Mexican female ancestors. The second document is a poem celebrating the "new" Chicana who fights for equality AND for her *raza*, a true Adelita. The following document contains the resolutions arrived at during the First National Chicana conference celebrated in Houston and attended by over 600 women. The fourth document is by an anonymous young woman describing how her own consciousness was raised and her eyes opened to the importance of female liberation in the Chicano/Mexican community. The next poem declares that for the true revolution to take place, both men and women must fight as equals. Finally, Gloria Anzaldúa posits that the Day of the Chicana will bring Chicanos to embrace Chicanas as full and equal members of the community.

## From *The Woman of La Raza*, 1969

While attending a Raza conference in Colorado this year, I went to one of the workshops that were held to discuss the role of the Chicana Woman. When the time came for the women to make the presentation to the full conference, the only thing that the workshop representative said was this: "It was the consensus of the group that the Chicana woman does not want to be liberated."

. . .

Looking at our history, I can see why this would be true. The role of the Chicana woman has been a very strong one, although a silent one. When the woman has seen the suffering of her peoples she has always responded bravely and as a totally committed and equal human. My mother told me of how, during the time of Pancho Villa and the revolution in Mexico, she saw the men march through the village continually for three days and then she saw the battalion of women marching for a whole day. The women carried food and supplies; also, they were fully armed and wearing loaded "carrilleras." In battle they fought alongside the men. Out of the Mexican revolution came the revolutionary personage "Adelita," who wore her rebozo crossed at the bosom as a symbol of a revolutionary woman in Mexico.

Then we have our heroine Juana Gallo, a brave woman who led her men to battle against the government after having seen her father and other villagers hung for defending the land of the people. She and many more women fought bravely with their people. And if called upon again, they would be there alongside the men to fight to the bitter end.

And now, today, as we hear the call of the Raza and as the dormant, "docile" Mexican-American comes to life, we see the stirring of the people. With that call, the Chicana woman also stirs and I am sure that she will leave her mark upon the Mexican-American movement in the Southwest.

. . .

And what usually happens to this woman when she tries to become active in the "Causa"? One would think that the movement would provide a place for her, one would think that the organizations would welcome her with open arms and try to encourage her to speak up for her Raza. One would think that because of her knowledge and situation the groups would think of liberation schools with child care for the victims of broken homes, in order to teach them culture and history so that they may find self-identity. But, NO. Instead one finds that this woman is shunned again by her own Raza. When she tries to speak of Machismo, she is immediately put down and told "We know all about it, there are many many books written on the subject." She receives nothing but censorship again. She tries so hard to say, "yes, there is much on Machismo, but can't you Machos look at the woman and children who are the VICTIMS of your Machismo?" She tries so much to speak up and instead finds herself speaking to deaf ears and a completely closed mind.

Then she tries other ways, perhaps to offer her skills and knowledge in some way. This too is difficult. If she does a good job, she will have to walk lightly around the men for she may find herself accused of being "Agringada" or "Agabachada" (Anglocized). To top this off, quite often the men will accept or allow and Anglo female to go in and tell them how to run things. The Anglo will perhaps be accepted and be allowed more freedom than the Raza woman. Through all of this one sees a discouraged Chicana woman. One that hungers and bleeds to help her people and is turned away and discouraged. What is to become of her? Will she be forced into being a skeleton in the closet that one does not want to see?

. . .

The woman must help liberate the man and the man must look upon this liberation with the woman at his side, not behind him, following, but alongside of him leading. The family must come together. The Raza movement is based on Brotherhood. Que no? We must look at each other as one large family. We must look at all of the children as belonging to all of us. We must strive for the fulfillment of all as equals with the full capability and right to develop as humans. When the man can look upon "his" woman as HUMAN and with the love of BROTHERHOOD and EQUALITY then and only then, can he feel the true meaning of liberation and equality himself. When we talk of equality in the Mexican American movement we better be talking about TOTAL equality, beginning right where it all starts, AT HOME. (272–278)

*Source:* Enriqueta Longauez y Vasquez, *El Grito del Norte*, Vol. 2, No. 9, July 6, 1968.

# From "La Nueva Chicana," 1971

The old woman going to pray
does her part,
The young mother hers,
The old man sitting on the porch,
The young husband going to work,
But let's not forget the young
Chicana,
Bareheaded girl fighting for
equality,
Unshawled girl living for a better world,
Let's not forget her,
Because
She is LA NUEVA CHICANA
Wherever you turn,
Wherever you look,
You'll see her,
She's still the soft brown-eyed
Beauty you knew,
There's just one difference,
A big difference,
She's on the go spreading the word.
VIVA LA RAZA
Is her main goal too,
She is no longer the silent one,
Because she has cast off the
Shawl of the past to show her face,
She is LA NUEVA CHICANA. (19)

*Source:* Ana Montes, " La Nueva Chicana." in Alma M. García, ed., *Chicana Feminist Thought: The Basic Historical Writings* (New York: Routledge, 1997), 19. Republished with permission of Routledge © 1997; permission conveyed through Copyright Clearance Center, Inc.

# From *Workshop Resolutions: First National Chicana Conference*, 1971

## Resolutions:

I.  We, as *mujeres de La Raza*, recognize the Catholic Church as an oppressive institution and do hereby resolve to break away and not go to it to bless our unions.

II. Whereas: Unwanted pregnancies are the basis of many social problems, and

Whereas: The role of Mexican-American women has traditionally been limited to the home, and

Whereas: The need for self-determination and the right to govern their own bodies is a necessity for the freedom of all people, therefore,

BE IT RESOLVED: That the National Chicana Conference go on record as supporting free family planning and free and legal abortions for all women who want or need them.

III. Whereas: Due to socio-economic and cultural conditions, Chicanas are often heads of households, i.e., widows, divorcees, unwed mothers, or deserted mothers, or must work to supplement family income, and

Whereas: Chicana motherhood should not preclude educational, political, social, and economic advancement, and

Whereas: There is a critical need for a 24-hour child-care center in Chicano communities, therefore,

BE IT RESOLVED: That the National Chicana Conference go on record as recommending that every Chicano community promote and set up 24-hour day-care facilities, and that it be further resolved that these facilities will reflect the concept of La Raza as the united family, and on the basis of brotherhood (La Raza),

So that men, women, young and old assume the responsibility for the love, care, education, and orientation of all the children of Aztlán.

## Religion

I.   Recognize the *Plan De Aztlán*
II.  Take over already existing Church resources for community use, i.e., health, Chicano awareness-public information of its resources, etc.
III. Oppose any institutionalized religion.

IV. Revolutionary change of Catholic Church or for it to get out of the way.

V. Establish communication with the barrio and implement programs of awareness to the Chicano movement.

*Source:* Mirta Vidal, *Chicanas Speak Out* (New York: Pathfinder Press, 1971), 13–15.

# From *A Chicana's Message,* 1972

There was a family in the park yesterday that reminded me of my family. They were all sitting around drinking cerveza [beer], eating tacos and listening to Mexican music. Then I noticed something that bothered me. A young girl walked by the table and all the men checked her out. It looked as though the Chicanas at the table got pissed off at their husbands because the men all giggled as though one of them had been scolded for being *manoso* [conniving].

A year ago I would have thought that those *cabrones* [jerks] were cute and very easily I could have been that girl walking by. I'm so glad that I don't need to be checked out to boost my ego. That is one dependency I'm rid of. Many of my sisters are going crazy because they are no longer sex objects. That really hurts me inside because I know we have more to offer the world than our asses.

The women who were at the table were pregnant and I have gone through that torture. I have been on both sides of the fence. As women we have been pitted against each other for the big prize . . . el macho? We are constantly competing with one another, even when we walk down the street we are trying to hold our stomachs in or push our chichi's [breasts] out. Believe me, that ain't a very comfortable way to walk, but we do it. Since we're little girls we're taught to flirt, then when we have boyfriends or get married and the men criticize us for being flirts—what do they expect? We are taught to use our bodies to get attention!

Who cares how we feel inside? Who cares about the useless feeling a woman over thirty gets because she is showing her age? Many times I have heard my mother say that she is old and stupid. What a waste of human energy for her to feel worthless at age forty. She has a lot to give, but she has such a low image of herself that she has no ambition. Christmas day I felt closer to my mother than I had in years. She kept crying about the mistakes in her life. Then I started hugging her and, of course, I cried too. Our mistakes have been very similar; one of them was trusting men. All of our lives we are taught to be dependent on men. Then when they mess us over we are supposed to remain strong and keep rolling with the punches. This is one Chicana who is sick of rolling with those punches.

As Chicanas we have a duty to ourselves as women first! We must get to know each other as hermanas [sisters] and open our hearts to each other. We must trust all women and realize that at this point in the movimiento "Chicano Power" doesn't include Chicana power!

Qué vivan las mujeres! [Long live women!]

*Source: La Verdad,* January 1972, 2.

# From "Empieza la revolución verdadera" [The Real Revolution Begins], 1971

The struggle is long
The struggle is much
Our men are few
Our women are few
Rigid boundaries of roles do not move
They make us separate
They make us fewer

Busily we race with the "man"
But time is too valuable to talk among ourselves,
        about ourselves
Understanding is assumed
Misunderstanding arises
Communication stops
And now we compete among ourselves,
        against ourselves
Thou shall not do
Thou dare not do

The struggle is longer
The struggle demands more
But seek the knowledge of all women
And seek the knowledge of all men
Now bring them together
Make them a union
Then we shall see the strength of la raza
Then we shall see the success of el movimiento
First,
Humanity and freedom between men and women
Only then
Empieza la revolución verdadera

*Source:* Anna Nieto Gomez in Alma M. García, ed., *Chicana Feminist Thought: The Basic Historical Writings* (New York: Routledge, 1997), 73. Republished with permission of Routledge © 1997; permission conveyed through Copyright Clearance Center, Inc.

# From *El día de la Chicana,* 1987

I will not be shamed again

Nor will I shame myself.

I am possessed by a vision: that we Chicanas and Chicanos have taken back or uncovered our true faces, our dignity and self-respect. It's a validation vision.

Seeing the Chicana anew in light of her history. I seek an exoneration, a seeing through the fictions of white supremacy, a seeing of ourselves in our true guises and not as the false racial personality that has been given to us and that we have given to ourselves. I seek our woman's face, our true features, the positive and the negative seen clearly, free of the tainted biases of male dominance. I seek new images of identity, new beliefs about ourselves, our humanity and worth no longer in question.

*Estamos viviendo en la noche de la Raza, un tiempo cuando el trabajo se hace a lo quieto, en lo oscuro. El día cuando aceptamos tal y como somos y para donde vamos y porque—ese día será el día de la Raza. Yo tengo el compromiso de expresar mi visión, mi sensibilidad, mi percepción de la revalidación de la gente mexicana, su mérito, estimación, honra, aprecio, y validez.*

On December 2nd when my sun goes into my first house, I celebrate *el día de la Chicana y el Chicano.* On that day I clean my altars, light my *Coatlalopeuh* candle, burn sage and copal, take *el baño para espantar basura,* sweep my house. On the day I bare my soul, make myself vulnerable to friends and family by expressing my feelings. On that day I affirm who we are.

On that day I look inside our conflicts and our basic introverted racial temperament. I identify our needs, voice them. I acknowledge that the self and the race have been wounded. I recognize the need to take care of our personhood, of our racial self. On that day I gather the splintered and disowned parts of *la gente mexicana* and hold them in my arms. *Todas las partes de nosotros valen.*

On that day I say, "Yes, all you people wound us when you reject us. Rejection strips us of self-worth; our vulnerability exposes us to shame. It is our innate identity you find wanting. We are ashamed that we need your good opinion, that we need your acceptance. We can no longer camouflage our needs, can no longer let defenses and fences sprout around us. We can no longer withdraw. To rage and look upon you with contempt is to rage and be contemptuous of ourselves. We can no longer blame you, nor disown the white parts, the male parts, the pathological parts, the queer parts, the vulnerable parts. Here we are weaponless with open arms, with only our magic. Let's try it our way, the *mestiza* way, the Chicana way, the woman way."

On that day, I search for our essential dignity as a people, a people with a sense of purpose-to belong and contribute to something greater than our *pueblo*. On that day I seek to recover and reshape my spiritual identity. *¡Anímate! Raza, a celebrar el día de la Chicana.*

Source: Gloria Anzaldúa, *Borderlands/La Frontera: The New Mestiza* (San Francisco, CA: Aunt Lute Books, 1987), 109.

## Notes

1. "Chicana" denotes Mexican American women, the feminine form of Chicano; the gender neutral form is "Chicana/o." The terms Xicana, Xicanisma, and Xicanx are used by some Mexican American feminists to reclaim their indigenous heritage by renouncing the Castilian "ch" thereby expressing their solidarity with oppressed peoples.
2. Mutualista = mutual aid society.
3. The Sleepy Lagoon trial was an egregious case of civil rights abuses that took place in World War II–era Los Angeles. The movie *Zoot Suit*, written and directed by Luis Valdez and featuring Edward James Olmos in his first starring role as "The Pachuco," is a dramatic portrayal of this harrowing and shameful chain of events.
4. This phrase is from the author bio that appeared on hardcover editions of *The House on Mango Street*. Cisneros responded to a letter from a reader's offended mother, "I was stating the personal route I had to take in order to become an author. To be nobody's mother and nobody's wife was not a choice for me, but a requirement" (*A House of My Own* 309).
5. The "macho" archetype is considered by feminists to be one of the less lovely legacies of the idealistic vision of a new Aztlán. Returning to a pre-20th-century paradigm of male–female relationships was never a goal for women.

## Suggested Readings

Brackett, Virginia. *A Home in the Heart: The Story of Sandra Cisneros.* Greensboro, NC: Morgan Reynolds Publishing, 2005.

Castillo, Ana. *Massacre of the Dreamers: Essays on Xicanism.* New York: Plume, 1994.

Cisneros, Sandra. *A House of My Own: Stories from My Life.* New York: Alfred A. Knopf, 2015.

García, Alma M., ed. *Chicana Feminist Thought: The Basic Historical Writings.* New York: Routledge, 1997.

Herrera-Sobek, María and Helena María Viramontes, eds. *Chicana Creativity and Criticism*, 2nd edition. Albuquerque, NM: University of New Mexico Press, 1996.

Johnson, Claudia Durst, ed. *Patriarchy in Sandra Cisneros's* The House on Mango Street. Farmington Hills, MI: Greenhaven Press, 2010.

Martinez, Elizabeth "Betita." *500 Years of Chicana Women's History/500 Años de la Mujer Chicana.* New Brunswick, NJ: Rutgers University Press, 2008.

Moraga, Cherríe and Gloria Anzaldúa, eds. *This Bridge Called My Back: Writings by Radical Women of Color.* New York: Kitchen Table/Women of Color Press, 1981.

Ruiz, Vicki L. *From Out of the Shadows: Mexican Women in Twentieth Century America.* New York: Oxford University Press, 1998.

Sánchez, Rosaura and Rosa Martinez Cruz, eds. *Essays on la mujer.* Los Angeles, CA: Chicano Studies Center Publications, 1977.

Vidal, Mirta. *Chicanas Speak Out.* New York: Pathfinder Press, 1971.

# Bibliography

Acosta, Oscar Zeta. *The Autobiography of a Brown Buffalo.* New York: Vintage Press, 1989.

Acuña, Rodolfo. *Occupied America: A History of Chicanos*, 8th edition. Boston: Pearson, 2015.

Anaya, Rudolfo. *The Essays.* Norman, OK: University of Oklahoma Press, 2009.

Baca, Hernan. "The Chicano Moratorium August 29, 1970. Still Remembered after 35 Years." *La Prensa San Diego*, August 26, 2005. http://laprensa-sandiego.org/archieve/august26–05/chicano.htm. Retrieved March 19, 2016.

Blawis, Patricia Bell. *Tijerina and the Land Grants. Mexican Americans in Struggle for Their Heritage.* New York: Knopf, 1972.

*Bracero History Archive.* www.braceroarchive.org 2015, Center for History and News Media.

Brackett, Virginia. *A Home in the Heart. The Story of Sandra Cisneros.* Greensboro, NC: Morgan Reynolds Publishing, 2005.

Bruce-Novoa, Juan. *Chicano Authors. Inquiry by Interview.* Austin, TX: University of Texas Press, 1980.

Burciaga, José Antonio. *Drink Cultura: Chicanismo.* Santa Barbara, CA: Joshua Odell Editions, 1993.

Carrigan, William D. and Clive Webb. *Forgotten Dead: Mob Violence against Mexicans in the United States, 1848–1928.* London, England: Oxford University Press, 2013.

Castillo, Ana. *Massacre of the Dreamers: Essays on Xicanism.* New York: Plume, 1994.

Cather, Willa. *Death Comes for the Archbishop.* New York: Vintage Books, 1990.

Cisneros, Sandra. *A House of My Own: Stories from My Life.* New York: Knopf, 2015.

Dick, Bruce and Silvio Sirias, eds. *Conversations with Rudolfo Anaya.* Jackson, MI: University of Mississippi Press, 1998.

Fernández-Armesto, Felipe. *Our America: A Hispanic History of the United States.* New York: W.W. Norton, 2014.

Fernández Olmos, Margarite. *Rudolfo A. Anaya: A Critical Companion.* Westport, CT: Greenwood Press, 1999.

Fuentes, Carlos. *The Broken Mirror: Reflections on Spain and the New World.* New York: Houghton Mifflin, 1992.

Galarza, Ernesto. *Barrio Boy.* Notre Dame, IN: University of Notre Dame Press, 1971.

Galarza, Ernesto. *Merchants of Labor.* Santa Barbara, CA: McNally and Loftin, 1964.

García, Alma M., ed. *Chicana Feminist Thought: The Basic Historical Writings.* New York: Routledge, 1997.

Gómez Quiñones, Juan. *Chicano Politics: Reality & Promise 1940–1990.* Albuquerque, NM: University of New Mexico Press, 1990.

Gonzalez, Juan. *Harvest of Empire. A History of Latinos in America.* New York: Penguin Books, 2000, 2011.

Gonzalez, Juan and Joseph Torres. *News for All the People: The Epic Story of Race and the American Media.* New York: Verso, 2011.

Gordon, Linda. *The Great Arizona Orphan Abduction.* Cambridge, MA: Harvard University Press, 1999.

Griswold del Castillo, Richard. *The Treaty of Guadalupe Hidalgo. A Legacy of Conflict.* Norman, OK: University of Oklahoma Press, 1990.

Guthrie, Woody. "Deportee. (Plane Wreck at Los Gatos)." © 1961 (renewed) by Woody Guthrie Publications & TRO-Ludlow Music (BMI).

Gutiérrez, José Angel. *A Gringo Manual on How to Handle Mexicans.* Houston, TX: Arte Público Press, 2001.

Gwynne, S.C. *Empire of the Summer Moon: Quanah Parker and the Rise and Fall of the Comanches, the Most Powerful Indian Tribe in American History.* New York: Scribner, 2010.

Hames-García, Michael. "Dr. Gonzo's Carnival: The Testimonial Satires of Oscar Zeta Acosta." *American Literature* 72, no. 3 (September 2000).

Haney López, Ian F. *Racism on Trial: The Chicano Fight for Justice.* Cambridge, MA: Harvard University Press, 2003.

Hedges, Chris and Joe Sacco. *Days of Destruction. Days of Revolt.* New York: Nation Books, 2012.

Herrera-Sobek, María and Helena María Viramontes, eds. *Chicana Creativity and Criticism*, 2nd edition. Albuquerque, NM: University of New Mexico Press, 1996.

Hinojosa, Rolando. *The Valley/Estampas Del Valle.* Houston, TX: Arte Público Press, 2014.

Hollon, W. Eugene. *The Southwest: Old and New.* New York: Knopf, 1967.

Jaramillo, Cleofas M. *Romance of a Little Village Girl.* Albuquerque, NM: University of New Mexico Press, 2000.

Johnson, Claudia Durst, ed. *Patriarchy in Sandra Cisneros's* The House on Mango Street. Farmington Hills, MI: Greenhaven Press, 2010.

Lattin, Vernon E., Rolando Hinojosa, and Gary D. Keller, eds. *Tomás Rivera 1935–1984: The Man and His Work.* Tempe, AZ: Bilingual Press, 1988.

Lee, A. Robert. "*Chicanismo's* Beat Outrider? The Texts and Contexts of Oscar Zeta Acosta." *College Literature* 27, no. 1 (Winter 2000): 158–176.

Leon Portillo, Miguel. *Broken Spears: The Aztec Account of the Conquest of Mexico.* Boston: Beacon Press, 1992.

Marín, Christine. *A Spokesman for the Mexican American Movement.* San Francisco: R and E Research Associates, 1977.

Martinez, Elizabeth "Betita." *500 Years of Chicana Women's History/500 Años de la Mujer Chicana.* New Brunswick, NJ: Rutgers University Press, 2008.

Mendoza, Louis. "On Buffaloes, Body Snatching, and Bandidismo: Ilan Stavans's Appropriation of Oscar Acosta and the Chicano Experience." *Bilingual Review* 26, no. 1 (January–April 2001/2002): 79–86.

Moore, Burton and Andrea Alessandra Cabello, eds. *Love and Riot: Oscar Zeta Acosta and the Great Mexican American Revolt.* Mountain View, CA: Floricanto Press, 2003.

Moraga, Cherríe and Gloria Anzaldúa, eds. *This Bridge Called My Back: Writings by Radical Women of Color.* New York: Kitchen Table/Women of Color Press, 1981.

Muñoz Jr., Carlos. *Youth, Identity, Power: The Chicano Movement.* New York: Verso, 1989.

Murrow, Edward R. *Harvest of Shame.* CBS News. https://www.youtube.com/watch?v=yJTVF_dya7E. Accessed July 1, 2015.

Nostrand, Richard L. *The Hispano Homeland.* Norman, OK: University of Oklahoma Press, 1992.

Olmos, Edward James, dir. *Walkout.* HBO Video, 2006.

Pawel, Miriam. *The Crusades of Cesar Chavez: A Biography.* New York: Bloomsbury Press, 2014.

*Plan de Delano*, Latinopia.com. http://latinopia.com/latino-history/plan-de-delano/. Accessed April 15, 2015.

Prescott, William H. *History of the Conquest of Mexico, with a Preliminary View of Ancient Mexican Civilization, and the Life of the Conqueror, Hernando Cortes* (online reproduction, Electronic Text Center, University of Virginia Library). New York: Harper and Brothers, 1843. OCLC 2458166.

Rivera, Tomás. *This Migrant Earth*, trans. Rolando Hinojosa. In *The Norton Anthology of Latino Literature*, edited by Ilan Stavans. New York: W.W. Norton, 2011.

Rodríguez, Alfonso, "Tomás Rivera: The Creation of the Chicano Experience in Fiction." In *Tomás Rivera 1935–1984: The Man and His Work*, edited by Vernon E. Lattin, Rolando Hinojosa, and Gary D. Keller, 81. Tempe, AZ: Bilingual Press, 1988.

Rodríguez, Phillip, dir. *Ruben Salazar: Man in the Middle.* PBS Home Video, 2014.

Rosales, F. Arturo. *Chicano! The History of the Mexican American Civil Rights Movement.* Houston, TX: Arte Público Press, 1997.

Rosales, F. Arturo. *Testimonio: A Documentary History of the Mexican American Struggle for Civil Rights.* Houston, TX: Arte Público Press, 2000.

Ruiz, Vicki L. *From Out of the Shadows: Mexican Women in Twentieth Century America.* New York: Oxford University Press, 1998.

Sánchez, Rosaura and Rosa Martinez Cruz, eds. *Essays on la mujer.* Los Angeles, CA: Chicano Studies Center Publications, 1977.

Schryer, Stephen, "Cockroach Dreams: Oscar Zeta Acosta, Legal Services, and the Great Society Coalition." *Twentieth-Century Literature* 60, no. 4 (Winter 2014): 455–480.

Smethurst, James. "The Figure of the *Vato Loco* and the Representation of Ethnicity in the Narrative of Oscar Z. Acosta." *MELUS* 20, no. 2 (Summer 1995): 120–132.

Stavans, Ilan, ed. *The Norton Anthology of Latino Literature* New York: W.W. Norton, 2011, 788–789.

Stavans, Ilan, ed. *Oscar "Zeta" Acosta: The Uncollected Works.* Houston, TX: Arte Público Press, 1996.

Steinbeck, John. *The Grapes of Wrath.* New York: Penguin Books, 2006.

Suro, Roberto. "The Summer of the Latino Comeuppance." *Time*, July 5, 2015. http://time.com/3945565/the-summer-of-the-latino-comeuppance. Accessed August 8, 2015.

Thompson, Hunter S. *Fear and Loathing at Rolling Stone: The Essential Writing of Hunter S. Thompson.* New York: Simon & Schuster, 2011.

Thompson, Hunter S. *Fear and Loathing in America: The Brutal Odyssey of an Outlaw Journalist.* London, England: Bloomsbury Publishing, 2000.

Thompson, Hunter S. *Fear and Loathing in Las Vegas and Other American Stories.* New York: Modern Library, 1996.

Tobar, Hector. "Finally, Transparency in the Ruben Salazar Case." *Los Angeles Times*, August 5, 2011. http://articles.latimes.com/2011/aug/05/local/la-me-0805-tobar-20110805. Retrieved March 19, 2016.

Valdez, Luis and El Teatro Campesino. *Actos.* San Juan Bautista, CA: La Cucaracha Press, 1971.

Valdez, Luis and Stan Steiner, eds. *Aztlan: An Anthology of Mexican American Literature.* New York: Vintage Books, 1972.

Vasconcelos, José. *The Cosmic Race.* Baltimore, MD: John Hopkins University Press, 1997.

Vidal, Mirta. *Chicanas Speak Out.* New York: Pathfinder Press, 1971.

Villanueva, Tino. *Chicanos: Antología Histórica y Literaria.* México: Fondo de Cultura Económica, 1980.

Wright, Greg. "The Literary, Political, and Legal Strategies of Oscar Zeta Acosta and Hunter S. Thompson: Intertextuality, Ambiguity, and (Naturally) Fear and Loathing." *The Journal of Popular Culture* 43, no. 3 (2010): 622–643.

# Index

*Woman of La Raza, The* (1969), 149–51

Women: Chicano movement and, 128–31; fierce women in Chicano history, 142–48; *500 Years of Chicana Women's History* (Martínez), 130; LRUP women's caucus, 131, 138; movement in the U.S., 138; single, with dependent children, 142

Workers. *See* Migrant workers

*Workshop Resolutions: First National Chicana Conference* (1971), 152–53

Work slowdown, 66

*Wounding of the India-Mestiza, The* (1987), 147–48

Xicana, 156n1
Xicanisma, 156n1
Xicanx, 156n1

Yarbro-Bejarano, Yvonne, 125
Young Citizens for Community Action, 92

*Zoot Suit* (Valdez), 55, 67
Zoot Suit Riots, 87, 106

# About the Author

Sara E. Martínez was the first coordinator for Tulsa City-County Library's Hispanic Resource Center and currently manages the Nathan Hale Library branch. Sara has a BA in Comparative Literature from the University of California, Berkeley. She did postgraduate work in Latin American Studies at the Universidad National Autónoma de México and received her master's degree in Library and Information Science from the University of Oklahoma. Sara edited the book *Latino Literature: A Guide to Reading Interests* and writes reviews for *Booklist*.